One
Reason

One Reason:

21 days to a New Beginning

Steve Schofield

Dedication

Many thanks to my wife, Cindy, and my three sons, Marcus, Zach, and Tayler, for supporting me—and putting up with me.

Thanks to Rod Roy for inviting me to breakfast that cold, crisp January morning.

I also thank Casey Lake, Sarah Loper, Michelle Carns, Doug Hinken, and Darcia Kelly for sharing your stories from the triathlon.

I thank the entire crew who organized the Greenville Triathlon (Kris Berry in particular). It was an awesome experience! The training made me appreciate our local community of Greenville, MI, even more.

"Diceman" (a.k.a. Faron Dice) and the entire smile.fm crew for playing inspiring music through the many hours of my training. I didn't start out listening to smile.fm while training, but by the end, smile.fm was a vital part of my training regimen. Thank you for your ministry.

Shannon Janeczek (PublishSavvy) for awesome editing.

Contents

Introduction

Swim

Transition 1

Bike

Transition 2

<u>**Run**</u>

Author Bio

How I Was Inspired to Write *One Reason*

It was January 5, 2013, when I met with Rod Roy for breakfast at a local restaurant. Rod inquired if I wanted to do a presentation to the local Lions' club about my first Christian devotional, *52 Pickup: These Are the Words I Give to You to Share with Everyone,* which had been published in December, 2012. Members of the club take turns bringing in someone to share an interesting story from the community. It could be an author, artist, or local leader.

As breakfast began, we chatted about what I was to discuss, how long the presentation would be, the format of the meeting. Later, the conversation shifted to discussing my second book, *Remember the Nails: 40 Days of Doing Something Uncomfortable on Purpose*. I mentioned another friend, Doug Hinken, who inspirational in helping with various parts of *Remember the Nails.*

Rod stated he knew Doug also and mentioned that Doug was coordinating a sprint triathlon in Greenville on June 1. At the time, wasn't sure why Rod mentioned this, although almost instantly, I had *that feeling* again; the feeling I had before my last two books. God was figuratively tapping me on the shoulder to let me know that I was about to embark on a journey.

As our conversation continued, I told Rod about the theme of my third book, but that it didn't have a story behind it. The general idea of the book was about a fresh start, something like a New Years' resolutions, or a pledge. The idea was to do something 21 days in a row that would help develop a new habit; mine was to start exercising regularly.

I had mentioned to Rod a couple of years before that I had taken a class and the teacher mentioned something working out year round (running, lifting weights), but that he took the first three weeks off in January. He said he would typically go back on January 22, which struck me as an odd day. When I asked, he told me the gyms fill up until about the third week of January, when people start breaking their New Years' resolutions. This is where I first heard that it takes approximately 21 days to develop a new habit. I'm not sure if there is any science behind it, but it seemed logical.

As breakfast concluded, I mentioned to Rod that he might have given me the storyline for the new book. As I walked out the front door of the restaurant, I felt a figurative tap on the shoulder again, this time a little more fervent. God said, "You should do the triathlon."

My first reaction was really? Really?! As I drove to work that day, as with previous prompts from God, I accepted the challenge, and wondered how in the world I would achieve it. The comforting feeling I had, as with previous books, was there again too, because God was there to help.

Besides, it was January 5. June was a long time away.

The Training Journey Begins

January – The commitment starts!

The same day I had breakfast with Rod, I found the triathlon registration website and signed up.

I'm not sure about you, but when I sign up for something, it's like signing a contract. This was no different. If I'm supposed to do the triathlon, signing up was the first step. I still thought, why would God choose a triathlon? I never did anything close to this, not even anything as simple as a 5K run. I wasn't sure how to train, or where to start to get in enough physical shape to complete the triathlon.

One thing was for sure: if God chose this activity for me, he would open the doors and give the right guidance so I didn't fail. The second thing was that, of my three books, this was the first time I was aware while performing the journey that it would turn into a book.

For anyone who knew me during my high school years, running was one activity I didn't want to do. My attitude wasn't the best, and my effort wasn't there either. I've often wondered if I could go back in time with the perspective I have today, things would be different. (I have shared this fact with my kids so they don't make the same mistake. I hope they listen.)

A triathlon is made up of swimming, biking and running. I wasn't worried about the biking or running; swimming was another story. I had a bit of panic, thinking about finishing the swimming portion. When I was young, I took swimming lessons. When the instructor said jump into the pool, like any kid, I ran and jumped into the deep end of the pool. For someone who couldn't swim, that wasn't the smartest thing. I had to be rescued. From then on, up to and including training for this event, when I was swimming, I would panic if I couldn't touch the bottom.

I knew to complete the triathlon, I had to overcome one of my greatest fears. A few times the day after I registered, I thought that I would probably get part way into the swimming section, and not be able to finish. Then what? Here are the things I would later realize that helped me get through some rough training sessions:

- God laid this opportunity on my heart, and I felt the sense to complete the event so that He could be glorified.

- If I chose not to meet this challenge, the opportunity to glorify God could be missed.

- I didn't want to let Him down. I figured he'd open the doors that would help me come up with a training plan.

It had been 25 years since I did any type of strenuous exercise. I had no idea where to start. Prayers that day included asking for direction from above on getting started with the training.

To help confirm this was a new challenge, our Pastor had just done a sermon covering Hebrews 11:11 (NASB): "11 By faith even Sarah herself received ability to conceive, even beyond the proper time, since she considered Him faithful who had promised." It's where God told Abraham and Sarah he would deliver them a child. There was one problem: Sarah was too old for childbearing. But God followed through on his promise, and Isaac was born.

This was God speaking to me through scripture. If he could give Abraham and Sarah a child in their golden years, he could help me swim, bike, and run. If this was truly God-inspired, He would not let me fail. I had to be patient, and I'm not as patient as I should be. I'm also proud and often think I know what is best.

I was a little afraid that people would probably just laugh, wondering why an old guy like me is trying something like this. Instead of focusing on my fears and unknowns, of which I had plenty, I focused on what I could do to start my training as soon as possible.

Knowing someone who could share their experience seemed like a logical first step. I needed to talk with Doug, who had mentioned that he had completed several triathlons. Plus, with Doug being one of coordinators of the Greenville triathlon, maybe he would take pity on a newbie.

I also consulted with some people who provide personal training. I received some of the best advice, to complete a triathlon, I would need to train for more than one event per day (i.e., swim and run training in the same day), for multiple times a week. Up until this point, all I had done was ride an elliptical a few days a week for 30 minutes. Doing more than one exercise a day, multiple times a week, sounded intimidating. That advice would prove to be invaluable.

My exercise goal to this point (riding the elliptical) was to say that I was exercising to help keep stress at bay, and increase my heart rate during the winter. Another friend of mine told me about a program called Couch to 5k. I'm not sure I was a total couch potato, but close. For those looking for a beginning program, Couch to 5K is a good one, and is a nine-week program overall. It's an app you can download on your smart device (tablet, phone).

The program integrates a combination of walking and running, while slowly increasing your time running each time you exercise. The program rejuvenated my desire to work out on the elliptical. I'm glad I had previously doing something, or the program would have been a lot more challenging. I made it through the first week.

As I continued with my work out on the elliptical, I finished my second week of Couch to 5k. I got up to jogging 1-1/2 minutes and walking two. There is a five-minute warm-up and a five-minute cool-down. I really liked feeling stronger.

It was January; I was starting to set my goals on completing a couple of 5k runs in March and April. There was a local 5K called the Irish

Jig, which was in March. I tentatively thought about doing it. The next 5k run was the Greenville Yellow Jacket Challenge, a local 5K that benefits the high school, and would take place after the point at which I completed Couch to 5k.

Things were going well at first. I was doing well with the cardio. I knew it wasn't enough, but at least I was on the right path, which would help with running and biking.

A couple weeks into the Couch to 5K, and swimming, I was feeling pretty confident and thought I would sign up for some spinning classes. I'd never done it before, but I expected to ride the bike for 30–45 minutes. As with any good humbling, this didn't quite work out like I expected. The class started out with 10 minutes on the bike, and then we were jumping while on the bike, pretending we were riding up hills. Then we jumped off and did an aerobic workout, where we were simulating skipping rope.

The class was supposed to last for an hour. I made it less than 20 minutes. I got so lightheaded and dizzy, I had to sit down. While I was recovering, a nice man walked by and said, "You feeling ok? You don't look so well."

I said, "Um...I'm not feeling so hot." They called a couple of EMTs to check me out. At one point, there were four or five people making sure I was OK. They brought me some cheese and a banana to help my body recover. This was my first lesson in nutrition: what you eat makes a HUGE difference in your performance. Everything was fine after about 20 minutes of rest. So I found my limit. I won't be attending an advanced spinning class anytime soon.

As I was sitting there, I laughed about this ending up in the book. The people involved had no idea of that at the time, but I was glad they were there to make sure I was OK. From that point on, I decided to start with simple bike riding. I'm humbled by those who can do spinning classes; YOU are in great shape if you can make it through one of those.

Up until I started training for the triathlon, I ate cold cereal every day for breakfast. It was like clockwork every day. I switched to eating oatmeal, which until now I thought was just for old people. This proved to be a good move. I've now given up cold cereal in favor of oatmeal. Someone explained the health benefits of oatmeal in great detail to me; I don't recall the details, but apparently oatmeal is better for you. I didn't need any more convincing.

The spinning class was a little setback, which also helped foster a temptation to slack off on my running training, as I realized I wasn't in good shape. But that made me even more determined to see this through. I didn't want to let our Creator down. He blessed me with this great opportunity.

I was able to ignore the temptation to stop running, because I was starting to lose some weight. It was only a couple of pounds, but it was a boost to my confidence. I continued the Couch to 5k program, and finished the third week. I was up to running 1.5 minutes, walking 1.5 minutes, and running/walking 3 minutes. After finishing the third workout, the text stated I would start running 1.5 miles in the fourth week. I hoped that before the triathlon, I could run 3 miles and bike 12 miles, three times a week.

I started biking more regularly, too. Fortunately, I was able to make it an hour each time. I did a few intervals; nothing too intense. I was happy just to finish the hour without stopping too many times. The instructors were hard-core riders, and part of competitive teams. I let them give me instructions, and although I didn't know half of what they were talking about, I mentioned to them that I would be happy to just finish the hour without stopping. Nonetheless, I rode the bike an hour a day, three days a week.

And then there was swimming. This was a separate task I planned on tackling, since I hadn't swum besides occasionally for recreation. Learning to swim for distance was the next obstacle. I contacted the local fitness place to see if I could join to use the pool. They were gracious and provided me a limited monthly membership just for the pool.

February – Starting to get in a routine

I was on my way to train for all three events. It was the middle of winter, the first week of February, so at least doing cardiovascular and swimming were the critical items, for a beginner.

After my first swim at the local fitness place, my thought was, *"It's going to be a miracle if I can swim a quarter mile by June."* I saw a friend later, who mentioned they saw me trying to swim in the pool. The comment went something like this: "I saw you kicking and splashing and trying to swim… nice try, but you weren't very good."

It was critical, but to the point, which I honestly needed to help me to become better. I also recalled the pastor's words about Sarah, in Hebrews 11:11 (NASB): "11 And by faith even Sarah, who was past childbearing age, was enabled to bear children because she considered him faithful who had made the promise." I know my journey wasn't going to be as dramatic as Sarah's, not by any stretch, but I had the faith to achieve my goals.

Being a task-based person, my focus was on training every day, and tried to do at least two kinds of training every time. My plan was simple:

- Couch to 5K on the elliptical
- Spin bike for an hour
- Swimming almost every day

At this point, I entered my fourth week running, and second week of swimming. This was a productive week of swimming. I went from swimming on my back, doing the backstroke, to using a kickboard. Using a kickboard didn't feel comfortable, but performing freestyle is recommended to complete the swimming portion of a triathlon. One inspiration this week was the other verses of Hebrews that we had heard, Hebrews 11:8-10

(NASB): "8 By faith Abraham, when he was called, obeyed by going out to a place which he was to receive for an inheritance; and he went out, not knowing where he was going. 9 By faith he lived as an alien in the land of promise, as in a foreign land, dwelling in tents with Isaac and Jacob, fellow heirs of the same promise; 10 for he was looking for the city which has foundations, whose architect and builder is God."

I still couldn't swim freestyle more than a half a lap in a swimming pool, which was dreadful. It made me wonder, but I kept after it; I had faith I would overcome it. Putting together a swimming stroke, with good form (proper breathing and stroke) is the goal for a triathlon's swimming portion. I had a healthy respect to those who can. Proper breathing alone was a challenge! Later on, I'd realize the number of stories that would come from my lack of being able to swim freestyle was also in God's plan.

Couch to 5k continued to help build my confidence, too, because the intervals were gradual enough to not scare me. The program is designed to take someone like me, who didn't like running, and get me to look forward to the workout. The next week, there was more running than walking. I peaked in the fifth week; the running portion featured two eight-minute intervals, which ended up being running almost two miles. Me! Running two miles! It was encouraging.

Then, I decided to get my own spin bike. I preferred working out in the comfort of my own home, rather than at the fitness center. I figured if I could pedal a spin bike at the gym for an hour after work, I could come home and do the same (or more). As it was, I was already doing the elliptical at home and enjoying it.

I learned that training twice a day, four to five days a week, takes a lot of time and energy. I overcame the hurdle of doing exercise on a regular interval. It's simply a matter of juggling everything else in life to continue to train. I admire those who train for these events regularly; it provided a new perspective. At this point I couldn't even imagine finishing, let alone trying to win, an event.

The next challenge to overcome in the upcoming weeks was traveling while trying to keep up the training regimen. I figured, if nothing else, I'd keep on battling. At the end of February, I spent a week not swimming, because I had to attend a conference out of town. I was able to keep up the elliptical, and even tried a treadmill. At this point, I discovered the major difference in running on an elliptical and a treadmill. The second day of traveling, I did 15 minutes on the elliptical, and tried 18 minutes on the treadmill. I was only able to run a couple of minutes. This made me realize: the sooner I got outside to run, the better.

March – Hanging in there

I returned from my conference, and training continued through end of February into March. I got a bit of spring fever. I always consider March 1 the first day of spring, although the calendar says otherwise. In the Steve Schofield book, it's spring then, even though there are usually several inches of snow at my house at that point. "It'll be gone soon," I thought. I wanted to get outside to train. At this point, the event still seemed far off. God continued to provide good health (and the ambition) to work out.

I felt led to start Couch to 5k over, but outdoors. Finally, the weather was nice enough, and a local lake had a path around it that was exactly 2.2 miles around. I did the first program, which started with five minutes of walking and then intervals of 1 minute running, followed by a minute and 30 seconds of walking.

After going around the lake the first time, I realized my pace was 9:59 per mile. I was really surprised; this was a serious improvement. I had done a 5k walk the first Saturday after getting back from my conference, and averaged 17 minutes a mile. I'm not sure that first 5K walk counted, but at least I had a place to start. When I told my wife about my running pace, she said "That's all? I thought you'd do at least eight minutes." I liked her high hopes for me, but I was a little disappointed. After a minute, I realized eight minutes a mile would be awesome! (Note: My wife ran cross-country and track in high school, and her times then were well below eight minutes a mile).

One thing that came around March was a title change to this book. I felt led to change the book's title from *Clean Slate* to *One Reason: 21 Days to a New Beginning*. I kept using the statement "One Reason" when explaining to people why I was doing the triathlon. I would say, "I'm doing this for one reason: God suggested I do it." Plus, it describes the journey well.

At this point, I had been swimming for a few weeks and really trying, compared to when I started. I was somewhat comfortable with my face in the water, but I still didn't have the rhythm down. I was a little frustrated, but pressed on.

Later in March, the weather was getting warmer, allowing me to get outside running. For someone who didn't like to run, I never thought I'd say, "I'm excited to get outside to run."

On the swimming front, I was able to get to the pool at least five times a week. The freestyle stroke was getting more comfortable, although the breathing was still challenging. I was hoping by mid-April I could run outside three days a week, and bike 10 – 12 miles. My goal was to be able to perform both exercises together in one training session. This would help understand how tired I'd be for the actual race.

I continually prayed for good weather, which in springtime in Michigan can be unpredictable. I missed doing the Irish Jig race, as we had prior commitments. And on the particular day, the race got a couple inches of snow. The temperature was about 35 degrees.

I continued to make baby steps with the swimming, but still couldn't make it a quarter-mile. One of the drills I found I was called a pencil drill. During this drill, you float face down in the water and slowly kick to see how far you float after pushing off the wall.

This turned into doing what I call "thirds." I divided the pool into thirds and worked on freestyle swimming technique in each area. Each time, I would swim four strokes, stop and breathe, and start again, remembering to touch the bottom. I was surprised to realize I could swim the length of the pool quickly. Each time, I finished 10 laps. I needed to be able to do 13 for a quarter-mile swim (I figured out later that 11 laps was enough).

I was getting more comfortable with my face in the water, although, when I get winded, my technique slips. On Fridays, I focused on drills and technique exclusively. I walked through the water, practicing four strokes, and a breath. It's what people call "muscle memory."

For the running portion, I finished the seventh week on the elliptical; it had me walking 10 minutes and jogging 25 minutes. I was excited to get outside and start training. I'd been slacking on bike training. It is one thing to ride on a spin bike, and another to get outside.

I was proud to finish the first full 5k (walk/jog) around the lake. Going that far was something I certainly had to get used to, along with adjusting to being outside running.

One thing I noticed after running almost every day... it's amazing where your brain wanders while you are running. When I finished one day, I thought about how parades end: with a police car. I could see myself being the last runner, and having my very own police escort (a cop on a bike, probably, at my speed!). I even thought of getting shirts made up that said, "One Reason – A Race of 1." As my training progressed, I couldn't believe how many times I used the phrase ONE REASON. It re-enforced that I was making the right move.

I started averaging between 12:30 and 13:30 minutes per mile while running outside. Obviously, that isn't breaking any speed records, but I knew when I was done, I would know I'd given my best. (If you realize my time is slower than I started, good for you). For some reason, the Couch to 5K app calculated my average mile time incorrectly. It was even slower than my wife expected! Interestingly enough, someone mentioned that same week that "sprinters run a bit, and walk a bit." It surprised me to hear that, because I was a sprinter in high school. Of course, that was several years ago, and I still couldn't see myself actually jogging 3.1 miles.

The Lord spoke to me in various ways this week: via prayer, through other people, through song, and even some examples of others training for the triathlon. At one point, I was pretty discouraged that my swimming technique wasn't coming together. You could say I have "swimmer's block." I wasn't sure how to proceed next, besides to just keep training.

Then I heard a song that reminded me of 1 Corinthians 10:13 (NASB): "13 No temptation has overtaken you but such as is common to man; and God is faithful, who will not allow you to be tempted beyond what you are able, but with the temptation will provide the way of escape also, so that you will be able to endure it."

God was letting me bend a little that week. But I got help, too. I showed up at the pool, and the wife of the owner asked me how it was going. I told her I needed some help. She let me know that they offered private lessons. Weirdly enough, the last name of the person who was doing the lessons was *Shallow*. Although I wasn't sure of the spelling, that was how it was pronounced. I laughed, and knew it was the right direction.

April – Avoiding discouragement

In April, I had a couple of weeks where I didn't swim due to a conference, and a pre-planned family vacation. At this point, I was pretty discouraged. I was training about 4–6 times a week, simply working on technique.

Our vacation was in Myrtle Beach. It was the first family vacation we had taken in years. Punxsutawney Phil had predicted on February 2 that the spring of 2013 would be delayed by another six weeks, so going to a warmer place was a nice getaway. It was a little chilly at Myrtle Beach; however, by Michigan standards it was warm (in the 60s and 70s). We rented a van to drive down, and it took 17 hours to get there.

When we arrived, we were pretty tired. Unfortunately, the hotel was not what we expected. The rooms were not clean, and we didn't have a view of the water. We called the place where we booked the trip, and let them know. They worked with us to find a different hotel, which had a room on the first floor, with an ocean view. It cost more, but it was worth every penny, plus that is what my wife wanted to do. Happy wife, happy life!

I remember thinking while on vacation that I needed a mental break from swimming. I was trying so hard, yet things weren't coming together. The race was two months out, so I still had time to learn. And I did get some exercise while we were on vacation. I ran on the beach.

When I run, I run a little, then walk (fast), then run. I can go no more than a quarter or a half mile before needing to walk. My wife tried to run with me. We went about a quarter of a mile, and she said her chest was burning. She said I could just continue on without her. I thought at that moment, all the months of running, swimming and some biking might be paying off! Compared to someone who wasn't running regularly, I *was* a little ahead. By no means was I ready for a marathon, though.

We got home from Myrtle Beach, then I was home for three days, during which time I didn't exercise at all. Then I headed to Las Vegas for training. I spent five days there. I didn't get any official training in, but my friend and I walked "the strip" three of those days. All and all, it was approximately four miles, round trip, each time.

After getting back from traveling, it was time to get back in the pool, and back to running and biking. I recall training a few days after I ran two miles, I timed the first mile at 10:04. I was so excited to 1) be able to get my time down to that level 2) not feeling like I was going to die from running too hard. One thing that helped was having an inhaler. I didn't realize exercise-induced asthma was common. Being able to breathe was pretty important.

The lower running times helped provide some much needed hope as the Greenville Yellow Jacket Challenge, a 5K race, happened about a week after I got back from the conference in Las Vegas. This was my first attempt at doing an actual 5K. The event started two blocks from my house, so I was comfortable with the course. By now, I was pretty much settled on a pace I could handle, which was around 10 to 11 minutes for the first mile, and 11 to 12 minutes on each of the second and third miles.

When registering the day of the 5K, I bumped into two of my old high school coaches and they asked me what I was doing. My old track coach reminded me that he couldn't get me to run in high school. I said I was training for a triathlon, and using this as a training event. They were pretty surprised, to say the least.

Running the Yellow Jacket Challenge was a good experience. I set a couple of personal records. The first one was that I jogged continually the first mile, without stopping. This was a lot farther than I expected I could get. Secondly, I set a personal record of 36:41 for the entire race. When I came across the finish line, the official timer said 36 minutes, 22 seconds. Either way, I was excited with both times, and — I finished a race!

May – Close to the event, keep after it!

It took approximately until the first week of May for the weather to warm up. We had an unusual amount of rain; in fact, the local river was at a 104-year record high. And the cold weather prevented those who were training to get into the water. I continued to bike indoors, run outside, and swim at the pool.

The reality of the situation set in. I'd been training for a few months and realized that my swimming technique still wasn't what I thought it should be. I was nowhere near able to perform the front-stroke. I figured as often as I swam, I should be able to perform the front-stroke. Back in January, I started by literally not enjoying the water, and I had gotten used to being in the water several times a week. I'd asked a couple of swim instructors to help out, and they provided me with some drills.

As my training continued, I could tell the swimming helped me with my better 5K times. I felt stronger, and had my fastest 5k training times a few days after the Yellow Jacket Challenge. The next day I went on an 11-mile bike ride, and again, I felt stronger. I had the fastest 10K time, according to the watch I used. I confess that I was so disappointed with myself after swimming, I took the next day off. I prayed hard to God for guidance. On my way to swim after the day off, a song on the radio had some encouraging words. The song's basic message was that Jesus is with you, no matter what.

Later in the day, a friend posted online that he had run and biked. I mentioned that if he could do a quarter-mile swim, he could do the triathlon. He replied that he wanted to compete in the triathlon, but was scared to drown.

His comment made me feel uncomfortable and shook my confidence. When I turned on the radio later that day, the DJ on the local Christian radio station said, "Who do you trust?" He read Proverbs 3:5-7 (NASB): "5 Trust in the Lord with all your heart And do not lean on your own understanding. 6 In all your ways acknowledge Him, And He will make your paths straight. 7 Do not be wise in your own eyes; Fear the Lord and turn away from evil."

It made me realize I was trying to plan for my own safety while swimming, and not trusting in His plan.   I'd been thinking for weeks about how I could prepare and plan to be safe through the swimming portion. I don't swim in lakes, let alone somewhere that I can't touch the bottom. That is what scared me the most. I couldn't swim a full quarter-mile in a pool without stopping. How was I going to swim in open water that was 20 degrees cooler?

There is one saying that keeps coming back to me: I can't let my fear make me miss this opportunity to glorify God, and allow him the chance to work through me. *Lean not on my own understanding.* By this time, in early May, I was ready for the training to be over and the day of the triathlon to just to get here. I didn't know if I'd actually swim the whole thing, but I was committed to do my best and have a clear conscience by trying.

Soon after this revelation about trying to plan for my own safety, we started to discuss in our small group Bible discussion Romans 12:1-3 (NASB): "1 Therefore I urge you, brethren, by the mercies of God, to **present your bodies a living and holy sacrifice**, acceptable to God, which is your spiritual service of worship. 2 And **do not be conformed to this world**, but be transformed by the renewing of your mind, so that you may prove what the will of God is, that which is good and acceptable and perfect. 3 For through the grace given to me I say to everyone among you **not to think more highly of himself than he ought to think**; but to think so as to have sound judgment, as God has allotted to each a measure of faith."
(I bolded the phrases that impacted me).

I kept these statements in mind quite a lot as I was finishing my training. My living sacrifice was the swimming portion.   About the second week of May, I was at a low point, thinking I couldn't do the swimming at all. I even woke up three times in the middle of the night, literally scared. It was all I could think about. I kept reading online about how other people were doing triathlons, and their swimming style.

One day, when I mentioned how bad I was feeling about my swimming technique, my wife said, "Don't worry about what others do. Just swim the way that is comfortable for you, so you can finish."

Another friend had more comical advice: "The one thing you need to do is finish on top of the water," he said. But he said the same thing my wife had; it didn't matter what my swimming style was. Relating this to Scripture, it was clearly Romans 12:2: (NASB) "2 Do not conform to this world." Just because everyone else does the front-crawl and that is the most standard style of swimming, so what! For my first triathlon, I just needed to finish, regardless of how it was done. I felt relieved.

After my wife and my friend gave me these kind words of advice, I took a day off to give myself a break from swimming. Then a few days later, I did 11 laps in the pool, all on my back, and I finished in 17 minutes. You would have thought I won the Lotto, I was so excited! Early in the week I felt defeated by my swimming technique. After hearing words of encouragement (that aligned with Scripture), I had my best day yet swimming. I didn't care what others thought or would think about me swimming on my back. If I was able to finish the swim portion in around 15 minutes, that would be 50% faster than when I first started.

From then on, my swimming training started with 11 laps on my back. Each time, it was around 16 to 17 minutes to complete the laps. Then I would do some additional drills from the swim instructor. Romans 12:3 kept my feelings in check. It states that we should not think more about ourselves than you really are. It made so much sense afterwards, for God to provide these verses to boost my training.

Now that I felt better about my swimming technique and could finish a quarter mile in the pool, I set a goal to train for all three events in one day. I had been doing two events almost daily at this point. I was swimming four to five days a week; running and biking a couple of days a week. I was a little apprehensive to do all three in one day, but I was determined to see what my time was.

My first attempt went well; my time was 2 hours, 40 minutes. I didn't push myself beyond my limits, although in the biking portion, I was about three miles into it and though, "What did I get myself into?" I learned a lot just from that first "personal" triathlon. About 2 minutes into the bike, I realized I would need a watch to help keep track of my time. Secondly, I decided I would probably need to get some energy gels to help replenish my body and I would need to eat properly.

The next week I performed another trial triathlon, and did it 20 minutes faster. The twenty minutes I gained was probably because I knew the bike course now. The first time I took a wrong turn, causing me to ride about one mile extra. Training on the course, as well as doing two personal triathlons for practice, helped me believe I could actually do this thing.

The one thing I had yet to conquer was swimming in the lake. Through my research, I learned that a wetsuit was recommended. A friend mentioned a place online where I could rent a wetsuit. This proved to be the best swimming advice I received. I ordered a full wetsuit. While I was waiting for the wetsuit to arrive, the water became warm enough to start practice. I first started swimming the length of the beach. If I could swim down and back twice in front of the beach, which was approximately 400 meters, that was the quarter-mile swim.

On my first attempt, I didn't wear a head cap. By the time I did a single lap, down and back in front of the beach, I had an earache in each ear. A friend explained that the cold water stimulates the ear drum, and causes earaches. She suggested I wear both a head cap and earplugs. I took her advice.

I was happy to be in the water, although I still couldn't do a full 400 yards without stopping. But I could do half, and that was beyond my comprehension just a few months before. Then the wetsuit arrived, and after a couple more times going to the lake without it, I figured I'd give it a try.

Before using the wetsuit in a lake, many articles suggest that you attempt to put it on at home. When I took the wetsuit out of the box, it seemed strange. The rubber portion was on the outside. "How am I supposed to get a wetsuit, when the rubber portion is on the inside?" I thought. After about an hour searching the internet and watching some online videos, I finally realized the suit was shipped inside out. I felt a little silly, but glad I figured it out.

The next day I went to the lake and put the wetsuit on. My wife was with me that day to help zip up the wetsuit. To my absolutely glorious surprise, I swam about 50 yards and realized the wetsuit was like having a lifejacket on. Previously, I had joked with Doug about wearing Swimmies to help keep me afloat. But of course, the rules prohibit any type of flotation device.

The wetsuit was a gift from Heaven. I was able to swim almost 600 yards (three times down and back in front of the beach) without stopping. I was so excited, I couldn't contain myself. When I completed the swim, I was barely even winded. The buoyancy the suit provided allowed me to focus on swimming without worrying about keeping my body afloat. (If you are reading this for advice on swimming, get a wetsuit and try it out!)

From this point on, I was so excited. The race day was a few days away, and I could swim without worrying about not being able to finish! The entire five months of training, and spending more time on swimming than running or biking combined, was a gift from God.

Words can't describe the combination of emotions I had at that point.

June 1 – Race Day

The day of the triathlon finally came. There were others with all kinds of wetsuits, some using the full-length style like me. This made me even more at ease. When we lined up, the groups were split into two waves, with 100 people in each wave. I was the last person in the water for my wave and took my time. I stayed about 20 yards outside the buoys and went at my own pace. About halfway way into the swim, I put my goggles on my forehead so I could see more clearly, because the goggles fogged up.

While floating in the middle of the lake, I was so excited about being able to simply be there. I took a moment to celebrate the peacefulness, and thanked God for that moment. All the months of worrying and training had paid off. The biking and running would be no problem. And now I knew I had more than enough stamina to complete the swim.

When I completed the swimming portion, the transition between the swim and bike went smoothly. I put my watch and shoes on, and started on the bike. With all that I had learned by doing the two practice triathlons, there were no surprises. I had bought a shirt that was made for triathletes, with pouches for the energy gels. Throughout the bike portion, I felt really good. There were two locations where I needed to refuel. This helped me keep refreshed and moving along. I completed the biking portion in around one hour (57 minutes actually), which was my goal.

I entered the transition area for biking to running. The only thing I did was change my shirt. The night before I had the prompt to wear a shirt my wife bought me, the saying was "Jesus beat the Devil" on the front and on the back says "with a big ugly stick." The picture includes a rugged cross. I was about a half-mile into the run portion, when a lady going about my pace said, "That is a cool shirt. A good conversation starter." I told her I was picking up my cross and bearing it that day.

This is covered in Matthew 16:24 (NASB): "24 Then Jesus said to His disciples, 'If anyone wishes to come after Me, he must deny himself, and take up his cross and follow Me'."

All in all, I completed the running in around 40 minutes. This was about the time I had trained for. The running portion was the toughest, because I had some pain in my midsection. I had experienced this pain about 1.5 miles into doing all three events, when I had practiced the previous two times. I figured it was best to have it checked out before I completed the real triathlon. My doctor told me I had two hernias, but they weren't bad. He cautioned me to use common sense when I was running. At least I had an explanation for the pain. The doctor didn't tell me not do the race. But if he had told me not to compete, I probably would have done it anyway... all that training and worrying was not going to waste.

About 100 yards before the finish line, I got a cramp in the inside muscle just above my knee. It felt like someone punched me there; I could barely lift my leg. But I could see the finish line, and I was determined to finish. There were some people from my church working the finish line, so I was excited to finish. In my excitement, I jumped up and touched the finish line banner. When I came down, I got a cramp in the other leg. I stood there for a minute and then walked to the post-finish area where they had drinks, fruits, and other healthy food to help replenish the participants. In my prior training, I didn't get cramps in my legs.

My sister later called me that evening, wondering how I did. She mentioned that during the triathlon, she was working outside, getting ready for her daughter's graduation open house, she prayed off and on. I told her about the cramps in my legs, and joked with her that she must have quit about five minutes too soon.

The exciting thing was my time. Two hours was my overall goal. I later found out my exact time was 1 hour and 59 minutes, 17 seconds. I spent approximately 7 minutes in each transition area. It was a nice way to end the event. All glory goes to God for helping me through this entire adventure!

What I learned from the triathlon

In the story, I shared several things I learned during my training. The most important tip: praying. There were many times I wanted to give up on the swimming portion, but God showed me, through song, scripture and other ways, how to keep going. The desire to glorify Him through my actions was something I truly wanted to do... and not let him down.

If you are training for a triathlon or another event, are thinking about it and not sure, consult with your doctor first. I didn't feel any pain until I did the two personal triathlons, which were due to the hernias. I only felt the hernias when I completed about half of the running portion. The swimming and biking didn't seem to bother them. The doctor mentioned the exercise was good for me, and to use common sense. His advice was: *Remember, you are not training for the Olympics*. Of course, if the hernias had been worse, he would have told me not to do the triathlon. (I later got the hernias fixed, but that is another story for another day!)

Here was my training regimen: Four to five days a week swimming in the pool (taking two days off a week; I'd take usually Tuesday or Wednesday off, and Sundays). Those same four or five days, I would alternate biking and running. I would swim before I went to work, then either bike or run after work.

I also suggest you get a decent pair of shoes, so your feet, knees and hips don't hurt. Get a comfortable bike, too. You don't have to spend a lot of money; it just has to be something you can ride easily.

My wife and I bought updated bikes from the local bike shop. They provided honest service and quality bikes. When picking a bike, I went with what they called a *comfort bike*, it's not as nice for riding fast as a road bike, but had larger and wider tires. I could easily average 12–15 miles an hour (I averaged 12.4 during my ride). It's not like the road bikes that get up to 19 to 24 miles per hour. I wanted something I could ride with the family after the triathlon.

When talking with the staff at the bike shop, they had good advice: "A bike you enjoy riding, you'll ride more." I chose the comfort bike for a couple reasons. It was more comfortable, and the price was a lot more reasonable. I didn't plan on doing any more triathlons, so there wasn't a need to spend the additional few hundred dollars.

The triathlon I did was called a sprint triathlon; it was a quarter-mile swim, an 11.8 mile bike ride and a 5K run (3.1 miles). This was quite a stretch for me, although obviously doable. In doing some research, many of the stories I read mentioned people worried about the swim portion. You have to take into account your experience level before swimming in open water. Local fitness places sometimes offer triathlons that include swimming in a pool, biking on a spin bike, and running on a treadmill. This is a good primer to see how you do before attempting the event outdoors. Looking back, if I had this option, I probably would have done it.

The Greenville Triathlon had plenty of trained lifeguards and staff who monitored the swimmers. I was VERY scared about the swimming portion. I had never done anything like this, and didn't have anything to compare it to. But now I plan to keep on swimming, because I enjoy it, and it is a non-impacting workout. Getting into open water before the race is essential to help relieve fears of what it's like. For me, it was interesting having weeds and fish around while I practiced. The swimming back and forth in front of the beach provided the ability to be in open water and if needed, I could stand up for any reason.

Target Audience for the Book

As with my previous books, this is a story God laid on my heart, outlining a journey God put me on, to complete a triathlon. It was not a full triathlon, but it was enough to really stretch me out of my comfort zone. The 21 poems are God-inspired and helped me along the way. It was rough at first, as always. He showed up throughout the training and of course, at the end.

One of the goals for this book is help those seeking to start exercising their body *and* their soul. Our bodies are temples containing the Holy Spirit. If you take care of your physical body and feed your soul (your spiritual body) with God's Word, you'll experience benefits you never realized.

Our world is so distracted, with all kinds of things pulling us all kinds of directions. While I was training, I experienced this firsthand. Almost daily, I had to make a choice to continue training when I normally would have been doing something else, like sitting around watching TV, playing on the computer, or in the case of the early morning training, sleeping. Taking care of yourself both physically and spiritually is a choice only you can make. Fortunately for us, God is eternally patient and waits for us.

My hope is that even if you aren't doing a triathlon, and you're just working out to stay fit, that you find something in the 21 God-inspired stories help you start a new habit of exercising, both physically as well as spiritually.

The theme of *One Reason: 21 days to a New Beginning* is simple. I'm looking to help individuals who want a boost to get started on improving both their physical and spiritual lives. After 21 days, if you don't feel it helped, keep after it. God will open doors and not let you down.

For me personally, having an event to train for was important in continuing my training. If I didn't have that goal, I probably wouldn't have been as motivated. Regardless if it's a triathlon, a

5K, or just losing weight, set a goal and work towards it. Seek God's wisdom every day, and enjoy the journey.

God bless,

Steve Schofield

SECTION 1 – Swim

As you have read, swimming was a huge part of my journey. God displayed his wonders so many times and blessings to encourage me and motivate me. One way was providing several individuals along my journey. I asked one of the people who helped me with swimming lessons to provide her story.

My first impression watching Michelle swim was amazement. She could swim backstroke, breaststroke, freestyle (aka front-crawl), sidestroke, and butterfly. Amazingly, she could float for several minutes without showing any effort. Selfishly, I thought, if she can do all that, she could help me learn the front-crawl.

During the journey, she provided the right amount of guidance, helped me with technique, and taught me drills that helped me in greatly. Michelle was very helpful. I'm so glad she listened to God and helped me!

CHILDLIKE
by Michelle Carns

Mark 10:14 (NASB): "14 But when Jesus saw this, He was indignant and said to them, 'Permit the children to come to Me; do not hinder them; for the kingdom of God belongs to such as these.' "

"Let morning begin," I thought to myself as I began to succumb to the rhythmic routine of cutting through the clear blue water ahead of me. Each stroke washed away the morning bleariness and lingering concerns of the day before. I usually kept time to a song in my head, but this morning something very unusual was happening; a movement on the edge of the pool kept piquing my curiosity. The neighboring swimmer two lanes over kept touching the bottom and pushing back up again every couple of strokes. When I finished, the struggling gentleman asked me if I would teach him how to swim.

His childlike faith that believed I could teach something he wanted to learn rapidly disarmed me. I agreed to the challenge, not knowing I would be the one learning.

The story of Steve's first swim lesson had me wide-eyed with terror. I could picture an enthusiastic trusting little boy being given the command to jump in, and the shock it must have been for him to watch the surface of the water ominously rise far above him as he sunk to the bottom of the deep pool.

Returning home that morning, my mind was asking the question: Where do I even begin? A scripture verse memorized from childhood conveniently made its way to the front of my thinking. (James 1:5 - NASB) "5 But if any of you lacks wisdom, let him ask of God, who gives to all generously and [a]without reproach, and it will be given to him." I asked. Recalling a snippet of something Steve told me gave me the first step. He mentioned how he could float on his back all day, but when he attempted to swim any other way, he would sink like a rock.

I knew what to do for our first lesson. His challenge that day was to swim a complete lap without touching the ground. Every time Steve was tempted to touch the ground during a lap, he was to turn over and float on his back instead. It worked! That simple lesson seemed to open his entire world when it came to swimming.

A few more lessons on survival floating, and breathing techniques followed, however, helping him realize he had permission to swim a race any way he wanted catapulted him over any existing obstacles still in his way. Steve's courage and tenacity went on to accomplish exactly what he set out to do, yet it was his childlike faith and humility that taught this heart how to be open to attempting the impossible in her own life once again.

Day 1 - Beginning

Scripture
Genesis 1:1

Poem
Think for a moment
There was nothing, everything was a void

God spoke, there was the heavens and earth
A brand new creation out of nothing

Only God, who is the most high
Can speak and make something so awesome

A crisp new beginning
Everything has that new-creation smell

When something is new
There is always a pleasant scent

Can you just imagine
Heaven's new, Earth new, everything brand new

When starting something new
It is a fresh start, something never done before

If the situation is starting over
It's a fresh beginning

Hoping to learn from past mistakes
In either case, God should be involved

From the very beginning
God was involved in every detail

As mere humans, we should remember God
He has been there all the time... past, present and future

Here is to new beginnings
God, this is a new beginning

I hand everything over to you
Please give me the strength to endure

When starting something new
It can make humans uncomfortable

We want to recede back to our old ways
Our old comfortable tendencies

God, you have a plan for each of us
We trust in your ways, not ours

Here is to a new beginning
And knowing I'm not alone in the Journey!

Amen!

Story behind the poem
When thinking of something new, or buying something new,
there is that "new" smell. It can be anything. New things have a
particular pleasant smell that helps remember how good an item
can be.

Smells are something that helps with long-term memory; at least,
they do for me. I hope you find this first day of the 21 poems
refreshing. If it's something you've been thinking about doing for a
while, you have made a big step simply by doing, vs. thinking
about it.

There will be a lot of people who will probably doubt that you will make it. Just remember, you have the Creator on your side.

Day 2 – Believe

Scripture
Psalm 23, 2 Timothy 3:16, 10:46-52

Poem
Believe, it's a simple word
It provides an emotional response of hope

When performing a task, it can be any size
The hope we can succeed helps us believe

When performing God's work
It takes a lot of hope before you believe

All that stands between failure and success... is believing
The world tells you there is no hope

"We don't believe in your hope"
"We don't believe in your message"

Our God continues to challenge us to move forward
Jesus performed many miracles

Many were present and saw the benefits
They still weren't convinced enough to believe in him

Many in today's world think they want to be left alone
Some don't believe in God at all

For those who believe in God
We try to be gracious, polite and loving

These are commands God gives us
It's hard and many days I don't know what to say

Then I am reminded, we have free will
It's a gift of love from our creator

In the end, Jesus will separate the sheep from the goats
The goats will be sent south, as sheep are escorted into heaven

On that final day, my hope is you believe in God
If you don't believe, that is your God-given right

Even if you don't think you make a choice to believe
You do make a choice

Amen!

Story Behind the Poem
There are those who don't believe in anything. There are also those who do believe, can't see what they believe, but have faith in what they believe.

Those who don't believe in anything are so paranoid about keeping those who believe at a distance, that it perpetuates all kinds of unbelief.   Those who believe want to convert those who don't believe. This causes the non-believer to be uncomfortable.
Both those who don't believe and those who do will eventually go somewhere. Who knows where, or when. Until non-believers are ready to believe, on their own, we can only hope that time comes before they are unable to believe and it is too late.

What do you believe? Why do you believe? What things happened in your life to cause you to believe in what you do? It's important to be comfortable with your choice in what you believe, because only you can control what you believe.

The One I believe in can choose people for His work. Your work might end up being trying to convince those who don't believe and help them to believe. Think about what you believe. Believe it or not, you will make a choice.

Day 3 - Boat

Scripture
Genesis 5 – 9

Poem
In the early days
The Lord made man in his image

And took a rib from the man
To make woman

He made them perfect
Adam and Eve walked in the Garden

One day a serpent came along
Tempting her with deception and lies

They ate of the fruit
Found out they were human

According to God's promise
They were set to die

As time passed, God was still with them
More and More individuals were born under sin

Over time, mankind got more corrupt
Nothing was sacred

Man's eyes were blinded
There was no pleasure they didn't seek

They forgot the Lord
Every man was evil in God's eyes

Except for one—Noah
Noah found favor in God's eyes

He, his sons and their wives
Were chosen to carry on

God commanded Noah to build a boat
The exact measurements were provided

Mankind in their blindness
Mocked Noah for building this boat

The boat was to hold two of every kind
That walked, crawled and flew on the earth

Along with Noah and his family
A simple boat to float in, while the earth was cleansed

God was sad he had to reset his creation
He started over with Noah at the helm

God protected them for a period of time
And when the journey on the boat was completed

The boat rested upon a mountain
Once the water receded

The door was opened
Every living thing was set free

It was a new beginning for Noah and his family
All the animals were set free

"Go forth and multiply"
According to God's command

Man's heart is corrupt from birth
We seek our own desires

But unless we seek God's heart
Our journey is for naught

God wants us to jump onto his boat
It will literally save us

His boat will handle the rough seas of life
As we roll from wave to wave

God will be a calming force
While the winds of change abound in our daily lives

With God and his boat
He is our refuge

There will still be turmoil, but our heart will be calm
Knowing God is the captain of the boat we are on!

Amen!

Story Behind the Poem
God led me to believe, after writing the Beginning story. The world
had become so corrupt, and God was disgusted with humanity. He
was going to cleanse the Earth, what He created. He even limited
our lives to 120 years (Genesis 6:3). Noah found favor in God's
eyes, and he was tasked to build a boat. It was a tool God would
use to protect Noah and his family while the rest of the world was
flooded.

After many days, the ark rested on a mountain, and all the living
things were set free. It was a fresh start for animal, bird, and
mankind. The eight who remained had to start things over.

This is one of my favorite stories in the Old Testament. If there was one character I'd like to meet, it would be Noah. I'm not sure why; maybe he could give an account of before and after the flood along with living 900+ years. It must have been pretty bad, since there isn't much detail mentioned in Genesis, besides a basic account.

Every time we hear this story about Noah, we should be reminded that God's boat can handle any size wave thrown at it; we just have to hold on. God is our calming force!

Day 4 – Break

Scripture
Acts 9, Job 37-41

Poem
Breaks start small
Some aren't seen by the human eye

These cracks become bigger
Causing issues in a foundation

It's only when the foundation starts to crumble
That we attempt to fix the crack

Cement can repair a crack
Nails can help reinforce a wall

The cracks in a soul aren't as easily seen
Through prayer and forgiveness, souls can be restored

Jesus told we will have troubles in this world
Everyone will make mistakes

Some will be small, some large
We will learn from them

In God's grace and mercy
He lets us break to the point we can't seem to handle

Only when we admit we are broken
Do we scream

"I need a break from life!
I need a break from stress."

Many think they don't need God
They think they can compromise

Some who aren't sure about God
Who are investigating God, see the positive things, but are cautious

The enemy makes sure there are consequences
Like anxiety or anger towards others

The enemy wants to keep you just hopeful enough
So you aren't totally broken, and then turn to God

The enemy knows that once we hit bottom
There's only one way to go—up

Some are totally dependent on God
God uses them to show his glory and power

Even when we don't know why
He can take someone like Saul and turn into Paul

He'll let Job become broken, losing his entire family
In the end, Job was restored to glorify God

None of us have any idea what God's plan is
We have to trust that he is leading us through all of our experiences

All things are used for good and for his purpose
The next time he asks you to bend or break

He is asking you to break old habits
Do away with an old way of life

When you accept Christ as your Savior
You are a new creation

The old, broken you is gone
The new has arrived

It takes us a while to realize that
God is the ultimate mechanic

He can take whatever, whoever, whenever
Whatever shape, no matter how broken

He repairs them using his tools
Love, Grace, Mercy, and Compassion

Man can't fix everything
God can! Give him a chance!

Give God a break
He has a plan for you

You just need to start with a small break - it will be worth it
Let him work his wonders in you

Amen!

Story Behind the Poem

During my two-week break from swimming in April, I kept thinking about it. I was so frustrated, and ready to give up. The enemy tried to move in and make me believe that I didn't need God, and I didn't need to follow through on his command of doing the triathlon.

Even though I wasn't making any progress in my attempt to swing with the front-crawl, I felt every day that I still needed to get up and do my best for that day. When I would complete my swimming session, most of the time I would feel dejected.

I got home from swimming one day, sat down and wrote this story.

God reminded what Job had to endure and later, Paul. God was still able to help both of them. Both of their situations were a lot more challenging than mine.

Day 5 – Cancel Button

Scripture

Genesis 2:2, Leviticus 25:2-7

Poem

We go, we stop
We go, we stop

Busy, busy, busy
Do this, do that

Interruptions abound
Day after day

Month after month
Year after year

If it's not to visit a sick friend
It's counseling a weak soul

Leading worship
Leading a group

The demands never end
There is always something to pray for

When there is a moment to stop
A deep breath is needed

Then, back in the fast lane
Serving God's people continues

Over and over, this pace continues
Until one day you reflect and say, "Enough!"

Our hearts just ache
We want to continue, but desire is sapped

We say, "I can go only so long before I need a break"
We need to hit the pause button

Press cancel to stop the action
On the seventh day He rested

Every seven days, stop your normal work
Reflect on God and what he provides

Man thinks he knows best and continues forward
Not following God's example

One day out of seven
God is not asking for much

It's for our own good
Even non-believers take time off

We need to pay attention to our pace
Otherwise we'll be run over by our own speed

Burnout, dissatisfaction, numbness
Feelings that will eventually come to all

For those who continue to ignore God's example
Press pause, press cancel, slow down

In order to revive and have a fresh start
Heed God's example of learning to rest

Sometimes, we need to slow down
To go faster in our journey

Thank you God for providing examples
How to refresh, re-start and re-tool!

Amen!

Story Behind the Poem
In our culture today, giving someone a year off is unheard of, especially in our busy careers. Our church realized that our pastor needed some time off. Our lead pastor had finally decided to take some time away. He had been teaching for seven years, and had not had any break.

I don't even begin to understand the call to ministry. As an observer, one can only imagine the things they hear and feel. The types of things I've asked them to pray for are pretty significant. I'm just one person! Imagine 200, 500, 1000 people laying all of their prayers on a pastor's heart. The burdens one would feel are enormous.

God provides examples how to cope with being overwhelmed in a fallen world. We all know that rest and relaxation is a must. I appreciate that our church board had the wisdom to follow God's example.

Day 6 – Cling

Scripture
John 3:16

Poem
Every moment in life, I cling to hope
It's like swimming

Every stroke forward keeps you moving
If you stop, you sink

In life, the world beats you down
Moment by moment

Saying to you
"You are not good enough"

The water we swim in
The land we walk on

The air we breathe
We take these things for granted

Every day, we assume oxygen will be there
Every day, we assume water and land will be there

When we feel like we can't do something
We must cling to the hope that

We will achieve our goal one day
A bank full of money can't buy hope

It can only buy temporary happiness
When the bank is empty, Hope fades quickly

The only thing to truly cling onto is Jesus
He came from Heaven, from perfection, to save all of us

He lived 33 years on earth
Not very long, really

His short time here was a lifetime's worth of greatness
His sacrifice brought us eternal hope

Something to cling to
Something to look forward to

If we only cling to our own vices
We would fade into nothingness

I cling to the hope of my Savior
The One who saved the world

Thank you, Jesus, for giving up perfection
Coming to Earth, and doing what you did

This gives me something to cling to
Every moment of every day

Amen!

Story Behind the Poem

The day before Good Friday, I finished swimming (or attempting to). During the entire swim, the person next to me was swimming using the front-crawl and breathing like I wanted to. I thought, God when are you going to grant me the skills to do that? You created the world, you created the water, and you brought people back from the dead. All I'm asking for is to swim like the guy next to me.

Then I had the word 'cling' pop into my head. During my swim, the enemy was saying "You can't do this. You'll never do this. You'll fail when you do the triathlon." More than doubting myself, I doubted the One who called me to do this would let me fail. Even if I failed, there will be a lesson for others.

I had to cling to the hope that one day He'd grant me all of the skills to make it through the triathlon. I was scared to death really, as I said. But I knew I was doing it, enduring the training and eventually the triathlon (failure or not!) for One Reason: Him. I wanted to do my best to not let my Savior down.

All he asks is a relationship, for us to cling to God, and not things of this world. The hope I cling to will eventually take me to Glory with him, forever and ever! Praise God!

Day 7 – Day

Scripture
Matthew 26, 27

Poem
One day, God laid the word Day on my heart
All day long, I saw the word day

Ever thought of the word day?
Every day of the week ends in Day

When we have special days
We've named them Holiday

When referring to nights, we say Sunday night, or Sunday evening
We don't say Sun-night or Sun-evening

The first part of every day brings a sunrise
The horizon bringing forth God's glory, the sun

When you see people
They ask how your day is going

When you leave somewhere
They say have a good "day"

When you get married
The bride and groom are told, "It's your day!"

Some people's names end in Day
The ones I know have made an impact on many

After a bad day, a night's rest
Then a new day brings a fresh perspective

When asking for a blessing
We say, "Have a blessed day."

My prayer to God goes something like this
"God, I ask for a blessing today

All day long, please help me through any challenges
I lay them at your feet, in the throne room

When a storm hits, please bring peace in the middle of it
Do not let the storm shake my faith this day

God, you are my foundation, my rock, my fortress
No matter what happens each day

I look to praise you, every moment of every day
Even when I'm having a down day, I try to praise you."

I pray all day long, handing every struggle to you
We don't know how many days we have on Earth

Let us make the most of every day
When the day starts, darkness retreats

You did something awesome in just three days
"How can you rebuild the temple in three days?" they asked.

You showed them in the middle of the day
Thank you for what you did for all of us.

I wonder what you thought those few days
For surely, you knew what was coming

First, you were welcomed as a King
A few days later, you were crucified

One day, you'll have two different perspectives
You will walk from this world into eternity

The next moment, you'll see Jesus
In one day, you experience the worst thing, death

The very same day, the very best thing, seeing Jesus
I'm sure it'll be exciting

I hope when you read this poem on an ordinary day
This helps you have an extraordinary day!

Ask God for a blessed day
Sit back and enjoy every moment... today!

Amen!

Story Behind the Poem
I wrote this on a Friday after one the morning swims. It was a GREAT day. I officially completed my first quarter-mile in the pool in around 17 minutes, which was a personal record. I hadn't been able to finish this distance without stopping. I swam on my back, but it didn't matter. The extra joy I felt just completing was very rewarding. Earlier in the week I was so frustrated I couldn't swim like other triathletes did, and I felt like a failure. That was NOT a special day.

From then on, I swam a quarter-mile without stopping, and then did some additional drills I got from my various instructors who helped me along the way. It was amazing in one week to have such drastically different days.

Secondly, a local person, whose last name ends in Day, is the local athletic trainer at the high school. He has been involved in our community for many, many years. He has used his extraordinary talents for thousands of athletes. We have been blessed for this person's talents. This poem is dedicated to him.

Transition 1

The first transition in a triathlon has the athlete go from swimming to biking. I practiced a couple times, the process of switching events. I didn't worry what it would take, or how long. The biggest challenge was unzipping the wetsuit. There is a long cord in the back so one person can reach the zipper. During my training, I had my wife help zip and unzip the wetsuit. I figured, if nothing else, she could help me on race day.

A lot of the people I talked with during my training said finishing the swim would be their biggest concern. This comment came from friends who can run 25k's with no problem. This didn't help my confidence.

After completing the swim portion, it took me just under five minutes to get the wetsuit off, put on my biking shirt, shoes and socks, and out of the transition area. I didn't think this was too bad until I found out the winner did his swim-to-bike transition in under 40 seconds.

My friend Doug Hinken was a source of comfort in this, because he could relate to someone training for the triathlon. Here is the story of how he got into doing triathlons.

Doug Hinken's inspiration to perform triathlons

The apostle James wrote "portion taken from James 1:2-4 (NASB), "2 Consider it pure joy, my brethren, whenever you encounter various trials...." It has never been a goal of mine to deliberately look for trials, yet that is exactly what triathlon has brought me to. In the process, I find that the progression toward a fulfilled maturity exists in a physical sense, too.

Only four short years ago, my triathlon-obsessed younger brother was the sole family exercise nut. Whenever the subject of his next race would come up, we all would roll our eyes and dismiss his misplaced exuberance as a result of being shot in the head by a BB (by me) when he was younger. But he wore me down. His persistence finally caused me to give triathlon a chance. I was hooked! He started me on this path of looking for enjoyment, even in the trials, that I pay money to suffer.

My experience in triathlons has reminded me that:

-- Hard work is its own reward

-- That trials are only temporary

-- That shortcuts don't end in reward

-- That to finish is most important, finishing well is better

-- That obstacles can be overcome

-- That if the mind is unguarded, it is prone to defeat

-- That keeping the mind focused on the finish line can get you through just about anything and,

-- A disciplined life can keep you from setbacks in your development.

I'm pretty sure that the apostle Paul was facing much more serious trials when he wrote the words to 2 Corinthians 4:16-18 (NASB), but this is how I feel at some point during every race: "16 Therefore we do not lose heart, but though our outer man is decaying, yet our inner man is being renewed day by day. 17 For momentary, light affliction is producing for us an eternal weight of glory far beyond all comparison, 18 while we look not at the things which are seen, but at the things which are not seen; for the things which are seen are temporal, but the things which are not seen are eternal."

Perhaps when I face more serious trials (the ones I don't pay for - or ask for), I will remember what I learned through triathlon: Finishing the race of life to bring glory and honor to the Lord Jesus Christ, the Giver of Life.

SECTION 2 – Bike

When I entered the bike portion of the race, a sense of relief washed over me. I had just completed the scariest portion of the triathlon, swimming. Biking was something I didn't think too much about, nor did I train very hard for. I simply wanted to complete the bike section with a consistent approach.

My bike is not setup like a normal race bike. It's was they call a "comfort bike." It has a wider seat and tires, and you sit more straight up. The race was comfortable, and after a few hills I had to get over, I knew the next hour was going to be peaceful. I spent time reflecting on the swim portion. I was amazed that I had actually completed, when I wasn't sure if I could. I've never enjoyed a bike ride like the one in the triathlon. I asked a friend from our church to document her story that goes along with the Bike section.

My Triathlon Story
by Sarah Loper

I had done a few 5Ks when I was 17 years old, but nothing really challenged me. I worked out at the local fitness center and had talked to Dave (an employee at the fitness center) about something a little more challenging. After many different types of weight-lifting workouts, I decided that the triathlon looked more appealing.

While training, it seemed like every other week I had a new injury. While some of them could be ignored, when I hurt my knee and then my shoulder, it brought things to a sudden halt. A lot of people lost faith in me and I started to lose faith in myself. I began praying to God and asked him for a miracle so that I could make this event possible.

I worked out for six hours a day, six times a week, and as you can only imagine this became very taxing on my body. I trained for six months like this and could do double the distance in everything at the same time. I felt very prepared for this race!

On race day, as I made my way to the front of the pack for my heat, I said a quick prayer and bolted into the water. When I hit the water, I thought for sure I was going to drown. It was too cold and my body just couldn't function in the icy cold water. I only completed the swimming with the help of God!

Next was biking. Apparently I hadn't been tested enough that day, as the chain came off of my bike while I was going up an insanely steep hill! And of course, I didn't have any tools to get it back on. I waited for about 10 minutes praying that someone would come by with a wrench or something. Sure enough, an older gentleman threw a wrench at me and wished me good luck while he sped past. It took me about five minutes to put it back on and be on my way.

Now that the biking was done, it was time to run! The part that I had been most prepared for was honestly the hardest. My muscles were so sore and my knee just wanted to give out. I fast-walked for the first five minutes to give myself a rest, and then took off at full speed to finish my race.

At about the halfway point of the run, they gave me a gel pack of an energy supplement. That gel pack saved my life. It provided just the right amount of energy to allow me to finish. I saw the finish line and I started sprinting, passing three people, and then I went through! I had finished, and had proven to myself that all things are possible with Christ who gives me strength!

Day 8 - Can't

Scripture
Mark 11:20-23

Poem
You are so busy telling me what I can't do
You remind me over and over

Let me remind you of something
I was given the desire to keep trying by the Creator

Day after day, morning after morning
Keep trying, don't give up

During the training
I grew comfortable with a few things

Four strokes, bring my head out of the water
Complete several laps without feeling tired

Comfortable with my face in the water
Getting up in the morning to swim

One morning, I swam and even ran for 38 minutes
When I got done, I felt so good

Just a few months before
I couldn't achieve either

The Good Lord works in subtle ways
As we focus on getting better

The enemy reminds of what we can't do
Over and over and over again

We get better at something than we were before
We move to other challenges

The enemy gives up
And moves onto other things

Everything that comes from the enemy
Is negative, full of half-truths, doubt, and fear

The Good Lord provides desire, hope, and goals
The total opposite of the enemy

There are days I just need to write down the differences
This helps both me—and the enemy—know where we stand

Good try, but you failed. God wins!
I still can't swim a single lap without stopping to breathe

I still can't seem to breathe without drinking water, too
If it's God's will, I will

All I can do is keep trying my best
Following his prompts

Doubt is a hard thing to overcome
Hand it over to God and let him deal with it

Thank you Lord for the reminder

Amen!

Story Behind the Poem
God gave me a real desire to learn how to swim. All I could think
about was what I couldn't do. It's the enemy who gets us to focus
on the negative.

I stopped for a moment, and realized I could do a lot more than before I started working out. This particular morning, I woke up at 4:20 a.m. and went to the pool to work on my swimming technique. I wasn't any more successful than any other morning, but when I got done, it was 5:50 AM. I realized I still had time to run on the elliptical for 38 minutes. Doing two exercises on the same morning was unheard of a few months prior.

The One I believe in commands the water; even walks on it when he feels like. I'll put my faith in someone like that to help me learn how to swim.

Day 9 - Face It

Scripture
Romans 12:1, 2, 3

Poem
Ever had a fear of something so big
You would avoid it at all costs

Maybe the fear started when you were young
You've carried it all your life

One day life was going along
You feel this tap on the shoulder: "You should do this"

You try to ignore God's prompt
"Please, please Lord, not that

It is a fear I don't want to face."
How do I know this happens?

It happened to me.
I said. "OK God, what is next?"

Day after day, training and pushing
Learning how to do something that I thought was impossible

Months went by, and the fear still resides
Waking up in the middle of the night

Doubt, fear, uncertainty creep in
The enemy tries to persuade you

"You don't have to do that
You'll fail and might not make it

Then what? Others will laugh, make fun of you
You could get out in the middle and freeze up!"

God has reminded me many times
"Who thought of everything, including what you are feeling?

If I thought it up, can't I help you overcome it?"
This brings peace

There is uncertainty in the process
There is certainty this will be used to glorify God

If *we* try to plan anything, or work around God's plan
It won't work; God will not let it happen

I put my full faith and trust in the Lord God Almighty
There is no swim, bike or run he can't handle

Anything he asks us to face, we don't face alone
We face it knowing the Creator of the Universe is on our side

He will use me as an example for his glory
I'm not sure how it will glorify Him or help others

I know that it's the one constant thing
This opportunity will glorify God

I face my fear head on, the day fast approaches
I've thought about it over and over

I'm tired of thinking
I'm ready to start doing

The next time you face something that seems impossible
Ask God to come alongside, to face it with you together

You'll be surprised at the outcome
I'm sure I will be in the near future

Regardless of the outcome, I praise God
For helping me face my fear and overcome!

Amen!

Story Behind the Poem
Before my first triathlon, there were times I woke up in the middle
of the night, worried I wouldn't make it during the swim portion.
I tried for months, trying to learn how to swim freestyle, or front-
crawl. Unfortunately, I was not able to get this technique down.
Instead, I do something called the water angel. I swim on my back,
kick my feet and move my arms (like making a snow angel).

When I was young and taking swimming lessons, they said, "Jump in
the pool." I jumped in the deep end and had to be saved with the
'hook.' This gave me a lifelong fear of swimming, especially in the
deep end of a pool. I had to be in the part of the pool where I could
touch the bottom.

Of all the things God has asked me to do, getting back to swimming
was one of the hardest. But now I can swim 400 yards in the pool,
without stopping. It still takes me approximately 16 or 17 minutes
to swim one-quarter of a mile. Overcoming the fear is not an
option, when God asks you do push through. Even if I fail, my goal is
to have a clear conscience, because I tried.

Day 10 – F.E.A.R (Forget Everything and Race)

Scripture

John 16, Matthew 6, Matthew 11

Poem

Forget everything and race
God will challenge you

God will test you
God will not let you down

While on Earth, life is a race
The race can be slow, medium, or fast

God will be there the whole way, every day
The enemy will be on the other side

Expressing doubt, fear, uncertainty
God is Sovereign enough to let this happen

He knows all things and how you'll respond
Praise God, Praise God, and Praise God

Non-believers don't want to hear these words
The enemy hates these words even more

A personal relationship with Jesus is all we need
Don't lose hope; don't give up on the race

One day you'll be surprised
You'll go farther than you have ever gone before

It could be effortless, or a struggle...
Regardless of the circumstance, God is there

The Bible states in Matthew 11:29-30 (NASB):
"29 Take My yoke upon you and learn from Me,

For I am gentle and humble in heart, and you will find rest for your souls. 30 For My yoke is easy and My burden is light."

Don't worry over anything or be anxious, as stated in Matthew 6:25 (NASB): "25 For this reason I say to you,

do not be worried about your life,
as to what you will eat or what you will drink; nor for your body,

as to what you will put on. Is not life more than food,
and the body more than clothing?"

When the blessings come from God
Appreciate it, knowing the enemy sees it too

He won't sit back being idle; he'll try to interfere
He is spreading fear

Jesus said, you will have struggles
John 16:33 (NASB): "33 These things I have spoken to you,

So that in Me you may have peace. In the world you have tribulation, but take courage; I have overcome the world."

Knowing the creator is on your side
He has died and raised again for our sake

That my friends is F.E.A.R
Jesus took on sin for all people, for all time

That is the kind of F.E.A.R I can grasp ahold of
I'll race a race with him any day -- I won't fear anything!

Jesus, thank you for putting your fears aside
Showing the world how to F.E.A.R (Forget Everything And Race)

Amen!

Story Behind the Poem
This was written a few days before the Triathlon. I tried my wetsuit for the first time and it was so easy, I almost wondered if I was cheating. I swam about 550-600 yards without stopping and I wasn't winded. The wetsuit helped me float so much I couldn't believe it. I even forgot to put my goggles on. This was not even comparable to the workouts at the local fitness place, which has a pool. It was a true blessing from God.

He laid the F.E.A.R. acronym on my heart. I searched online http://bit.ly/1ccGTsQ and nothing mentioned 'race.' There were 27 other definitions, but nothing with race. I was excited I could not wait for the day of the triathlon.

It takes something special to surprise me, I was definitely surprised! And then I remembered the sleepless nights, worrying over nothing. It made me smile and one of the things I remember most from the training.

Additionally, my wife witnessed this event, took pictures and sent them to my oldest son, who was in Kandahar, Afghanistan at the time, which made this moment special.

Our life is a race with Jesus. If we join the race with him, things will never be the same.

Day 11 – Helpless

Scripture
2 Corinthians 12:1-10, Job 37-41

Poem
It's been three nights in a row
I wake up scared beyond belief

Asking the simple question, "Why me?
Why have you given me this task?

What good can come of it?"
I've been at this routine for several months

The outcome is the same: defeat
The harder I try, the more I fail

I can't recall the last time
I wanted to succeed at something so bad

Paul says in our weakness, you are strong
You must be really strong, right now, I feel really weak

I try, panic and stop
In life, we try once, fail, try again, and fail once more

My hope is fading fast
I want to just give up, but can't

The little voice inside me says "Keep going!"
It's the one reason why I keep going

The time is quickly approaching
When I have to do this for real

"God, I cry out, asking "Why?" Then I remember...
Others in my life are going through the same kind of fear

For a different reason, it's way more serious
My fear is from a simple failure

Their fear comes from "How long will I live?
Or will I live?" They lean on you more than ever for comfort

I know you are there, you've answered before
You've shown your glory so many times, I can't count

The passion to overcome this one thing is great
So much so, I can't think of anything else

God, I feel so helpless
On one side, I get mad and want to lash out

Getting mad feels good for a moment
Moments later remorse sets in, then I feel sad

I sit here wondering, why me?
In God's time, he'll show me the reason

He has before and will again
God, I have ultimate faith you'll see this through

I don't know the outcome or impact
I know I'm scared, and lean on you with all my worth

Not only do you create the emotion
Words can't describe the emotion, that in itself shows your power

I'll do my best and keep praying.
The day I least expect it

I'll be able to overcome my fear.
In the meantime, I'll boast about what I'm scared about.

I leave you with this prayer:
"Oh great Father, Creator of all You control the seas, the sun and

Everything else, at your very breath, entire galaxies are formed
With this limitless power, we are nothing

We are a grain of sand.
I hand over my fear and doubt of the unknown

I leave at your feet in the throne room
Not only can you handle you, you will handle it

I have faith this will occur, in your time
In the meantime, I ask for continue patience

Guidance, strength, and love.
Be with me and others in my life.

Help them overcome the fear, we hand it all to you.
Thank you for testing me, keeping me weak

So you are strong, for your glory!"

Amen!

Story Behind the Poem
About three weeks before the triathlon, a good friend posted online
that the water temperature at the race course was 66 degrees.
That didn't seem too bad, but at that point, I couldn't coordinate
time to go and swim the course. Knowing I could do it would greatly
relieve my fear of being unable to touch the bottom.

I've been able to overcome the fear of biking and running together, even going for 2 hours and 40 minutes without slowing down during my first practice triathlon. My body was a little sore afterwards, but nothing too bad.

I have several people in my life who are struggling with cancer, and other unknowns. These people are believers, yet I'm sure they truly feel the helplessness I did; probably more. The least I can do is share my story God laid on my heart this particular day.

Day 12 – Honey and Vinegar

Scripture
1 Corinthians 13, Matthew 18:21-35, Matthew 21:12-22

Poem
One is sweet
One is sour

One brings happiness
One brings sadness

Situations in life are like honey and vinegar
Some are nice, some are not

Think of your last challenge in life
How did you approach it?

With a smile? A frown?
Others will notice how you act and how you speak

The idea to work on something together
Not to make others feel they have to, but motivate them to want to

The goal when approaching something is to be like honey
It tastes good, looks appealing and brings joy

Do not be like vinegar,
This will do nothing good for anyone as time passes

The hope is that people remember you more for your honey
Our Savior died many years ago

He is remembered as a perfect man, who knew no sin
His actions spoke as loud as his words

Just like honey and vinegar
Jesus's actions were more like honey

But on occasion, he acted like vinegar
Be like Jesus and strive to take the high road

Strive to be humble and sweet in times of turmoil
When the next challenging situation comes

Be like honey, you'll notice a difference
People will respond more openly

Do you want to be like honey or vinegar?
Our Savior showed us the proper way and spoke the truth

Our action is to strive to be more like him!

Amen!

Story Behind the Poem

My story was inspired by working on a complex issue
troubleshooting with multiple parties. When working with
individuals, there were moments and communication challenges as
well between all parties involved. This situation had multiple
parties, who are competitors. As we worked through the
troubleshooting process, there were multiple times each party
indicated the problem was with the other party's product.

During one of the issues we were investigating, I displayed some
frustration. One of my friends suggested my approach should be
more like "honey" than "vinegar." Patience and kindness
contributes to resolve. This was a good opportunity to learn
through this situation was appreciated because my personality is
more direct, which is perceived negatively (aka, vinegar).

God reminded me in 1 Corinthians 13 "Love," that showing patience, kindness (honey) will always get you further in life than being blunt (vinegar) and direct (vinegar).

Day 13 – Out

Scripture
Romans 2:8, Luke 22:42, James 3, Philippians 2:1-18

Poem
Ever been involved in something
You wanted out of, to be done with?

How bad did it feel?
Did you obsess over it so much

That it drove you crazy?
Were you on the verge of too much anxiety?

You knew better, but ignored the truth
All you wanted was your way and nothing else

You didn't care about other people
You didn't care what they were going through

All you wanted was out of the situation
Not enough patience, time, or money could solve it

All you wanted was relief from the stress
A diversion from the reality of the situation

You just want the uncomfortable feeling
And the people causing it to go away

The Lord hung on the cross for six hours
One cannot imagine how bad it was; I'm sure he wanted out

I imagine for a moment, being 100% human and 100% divine
If there was ANY way to avoid it, he would have

He was willing to go through such agony for us
When we have something that causes us stress

We need to hand over our troubles sooner
It is really hard as humans to handle adversity

We always seek temporary relief
We want the problem to disappear or be someone else's

Trusting God in situations like this is harder than ever
As humans we love to pick and choose what we trust in him

If we can handle it, we don't bother him, nor need his trust
When something harder comes along, we expect him to step up

When we have problems, big or small
This should be our prayer

"Lord, I come to you with this feeling
I'm 100% sure I can't control it myself and I'm feeling anxious

One part of me knows better, the emotions are raging
They want to take over and not let experience and reason
have a say

But I know better, and I understand what is right
As 100% human, I trust in your results - not mine

I've experienced them both in the past
I've seen your power, grace and mercy

I crave that feeling to help block this angst
I lay these feelings of anxiety at your feet

I know you work in your time, and not ours.
Even as I'm yearning to have relief

God, you say praise you at all times
I genuinely praise you, thank you for the test

I'm not sure I'm passing it, but praise you none the less
I say this and hand over the entire situation to you

As only you can resolve and forget it."

Amen!

Story Behind the Poem

I was involved in a dispute with some close loved ones. I had drunk coffee earlier in the day and the caffeine made me edgy (note: I don't drink caffeinated drinks, so a little caffeine gives me energy). When the discussion started, it was civil. Then I became defensive and negative, and I just wanted out the situation.

Reflecting back, I was wrong to act in such an immature fashion. I was supposed to be the role model and acted like a spoiled brat instead. All I could think of was myself, and wanting to hand over the angst I felt at the time.

As my walk with the Lord grows deeper, I find there are times that I slip back into the "old Steve." This is someone who was defensive and negative, and probably a bit immature. I have regrets about how I handle things sometimes. Emotions are powerful and sometimes, even though we know better, we let them get the best of us. Luckily, we can go to sleep and wake up refreshed, see a new beginning to the day and understand where our emotions came from.

I realize God will lead us through any storm of life. We just need to trust him and not try to steer the ship while the seas are rough.

When the emotions are raging, it's hard to let go of the wheel. We are forgiven: a clean slate in God's eyes. We just forget sometimes and need reminding.

Day 14 – Show Up and Try

Scripture
Jeremiah 29:11

Poem
Man has expectations when trying to achieve a goal
Man expects things to go a certain way

If they don't, adjustments are made
A tweak here, a modification there

Do some research to find better ways
Or different methods to succeed

Over and over, day after day
Morning after morning of failures

Can you imagine doing something you love so much
That you fail 10,000 times trying?

On that next try, after so many failures
Success! Achievement!

It takes patience; passion and willing to succeed
All of these traits come from our Heavenly Father

In Jeremiah 29:11 (NASB): "11 'For I know the plans
that I have for you,' declares the Lord,

'Plans for welfare and not for
calamity to give you a future and a hope.' "

If it's his plan, we'll succeed at our goal
All we can do is show up and try

We should be humble in our pursuit
And not let the enemy convince us otherwise

Oh Lord, many days have passed
Many failures have happened

You continue to provide persistence
You continue to provide opportunity

Help me, Oh Lord, for I want to succeed in your name
When I try doing this myself, I fail miserably

I cannot do this alone
I need your help and guidance

Every breath comes from you, Oh Lord
I will drown without your guidance and teachings

Thank you again for giving me the ability
Thank you for letting me show up and try

I'm waiting for that 10,001st time when I succeed
I'm not sure what I'll do when that time comes

But I will know it's one more gift you have given me
And I will thank you for your word, your guidance, and willingness
to invest in me

When the dawn comes
It is another gift you give the world

Just as you did with your son
Who died and saved all of us

Amen!

Story Behind the Poem

When I first started trying to swim the front crawl, almost every morning I had been trying to swim at the local fitness place. I was comfortable with four strokes, then exhaling, but it was the inhaling I couldn't do and the result was that I stopped swimming. I was so close to being able to perform the front-crawl, or so I thought. This example reminded me almost like a baby who is about ready to crawl. They get up on all fours, rock back and forth, but do not crawl.

As a parent, you know it's not long. This illustration is the same: good form, exhaling. The problem is the inhaling water up my nose. Who would think inhaling oxygen would be so hard?

I've not quite figured out everything. I show up with hope, yet to realize I still can't quite put it all together.

When driving home this particular morning, although my hope was diminished, the words came to me: "In his time you'll get it, keep after it." So I waited patiently and showed up to try. In God's time, I'll be able to put everything together and 'crawl' back and forth in the water.

Transition 2

Just before entering the second transition of the triathlon, at the end of the bike portion, there was a large hill we had to descend. It required everyone to make a sharp 90-degree left turn. I used both my front and back brakes, so I wouldn't go too fast coming into the turn. After reaching the bottom, I had approximately a half-mile left to ride, which was almost like a victory lap.

I was not worn out yet, so I was excited to get to the last portion: running. As mentioned earlier, the transition between biking and running was much easier than the swim-to-bike transition. All I did was change into a t-shirt.

I was also excited to complete the run portion, because my youngest son Tayler was working at a help station at the two-mile marker. I knew when I saw him that I would only have about 12 minutes left.

Listening to God and My Triathlon Story
by Casey Lake

I don't really believe in "gut feelings," "coincidences," things that happen "by chance," etc. I do believe you can have feelings that make it seem like these things really happen, though. What I do believe is that when we have the feelings that give the impression of a coincidence, or one of the others I mentioned, when this is actually God speaking to you.

We know that God has not spoken audibly to anyone on earth since about 90 A.D. when he spoke to the Apostle John, while he was writing the last book of the Bible, Revelation. Now, saying that, God does still speak to us through the feelings I mentioned above. When we have that "gut feeling" and think that something should be one way, or think our gut is telling us we should or should not do something; that is actually God speaking to us. The key here, is to LISTEN...

This brings me to a time, when I had all sorts of gut feelings telling me something. The problem I had was with the listening part. A very valuable lesson was learned from God speaking to me through various gut feelings, coincidences, and chances.

I had a crazy idea to try my hand at a triathlon. I had been running, in order to get into better shape and lose a few pounds, for about a year. I was actually getting into pretty good shape. I even ran some 5k races around the area. I was running a lot of miles at that time. Looking back, not training for the swim part (which for this race was a half-mile) or the bike part of the triathlon probably was not the best plan. Unfortunately, I had the attitude of, "I have run 2 marathons and a bunch of other races. I can swim and bike...no problem." This was my over-confidence situation number one.

The problem started the early morning hours of September 6, 2008. I had to get an early start in order to get to pick up my race packet and set up my staging area. We could start doing this at 5:30 a.m., and due to the large number of participants, it was recommended to get there as early as possible. Start time for the race was set for 7:00 a.m.

I had packed my bag the night before with all my race gear, which included a shirt, running shorts, bike helmet, Gatorade, towel, and Vaseline (runners will know what this is for), as well as a few other miscellaneous items. I got up at 4:00 a.m., ate a granola bar and had a cup of coffee; grabbed my gear bag, put on some flip-flops, and was on my way. I had put my bike in the van the night before.

As I made my way, it hit me. I did not put my running shoes in my bag. I had originally planned on wearing them to the race, then taking them off and putting them in the staging area, since the first leg of the race was swimming. Unfortunately, I was not thinking real clearly when I left the house since it was so early in the morning!

My thought was, "Oh man… I forgot my shoes." At that point, I was 15 miles from home. I began to compute how long it would take me to turn around to get my shoes and make it back to the point I was currently. In all, it would be about 25-30 minutes. That put me at 5:20 a.m., just 10 minutes before the staging area opened. I did not have to be there as soon as it opened, but wanted to be there in plenty of time. I turned around and made my way back home to get my running shoes. This was the first gut feeling to take note of.

I made it back home, got my shoes, threw them on top of my bag (which was unzipped) and was on my way. Full disclosure here: I probably did not obey ALL the traffic laws that morning. As I neared the race area, I thought I knew the streets well enough to get to the parking area, which was a few blocks away. This was over-confidence situation number two.

At some point I obviously missed a turn. I ended up near the hospital, which was NOT near the staging area. I was now lost. This was the second gut feeling to take note of.

I started to think to myself that maybe forgetting my shoes and now getting lost was a sign. Luckily, I saw a couple of cars going the opposite direction, with bikes on their bike racks. I thought, "They have to be going to the race," so I turned around and followed them. This was the first smart thing I had done all morning, because they took me right to the parking area that I needed to be at.

At this point it was close to 5:45, and I still had to find a parking spot, walk to the race packet pick-up area, then make my way to the (now VERY full and busy) staging area to set up my bike and my transition area. I had time, but did have to pick up the pace, which did not settle my already-stressed nerves.

I parked, got my bike and bag out, and was on my way. For some reason, I decided to leave my flip flops in the van and go barefoot. I walked my bike to the packet pick-up, and got my race info and packet. I went through the arm and leg marking area. Now that this was done, I could get to the staging area, and hope I could find a spot to set up.

I did find a nice spot on the first bike rack. I thought to myself, "Well, my day is looking up, this is actually a great spot." That thought would quickly fade. I placed my bike on the rack as directed, then began pulling items out of my bag to put them in my area. Shirt, check. Shorts, check. Helmet, check. Gatorade, check. Shoes, no. There was my left shoe...where was my right shoe? This was the third gut feeling to take note of.

I started to replay the morning's events over in my head. I knew I put both shoes in the van after I returned home. It must have fallen out in my van, when I threw them in there in such a hurry. Well, I couldn't run a race with one shoe, so I needed to get back to the van. When I got there, I opened the side door; no shoe. I looked all over the van; no shoe. I retraced my steps from my van, to the packet pick-up area, and then to my staging area; no shoe! At that point, I actually just started wandering around in a daze, not knowing what to do.

It was starting to be daylight, and was about 15 minutes before race time. The DJ was now playing music, and thanking race sponsors, and giving directions to everyone. I could hear the noise coming from speakers but was not really paying attention to what was actually being said. As I was wandering and hoping to stumble upon a right shoe, I heard the DJ say, "If anyone has lost a shoe, we have it." It really did not register at first, but a few seconds later, I thought, "Did he just say what I think he said?" At this point, I knew I had to investigate to see if it was my shoe.

But I had no idea where the DJ was. Luckily, I quickly found someone that had a two- way radio who looked like they were working the race. I approached them and asked them if they could tell me where the DJ was. They radioed to someone and found out that it was actually on my way back to where my bike was. My shoe had been located. I took my shoe to the staging area, left it there and went to the starting area for the swim.

They had heats of 250 swimmers leaving every four minutes. My heat was at 7:20 a.m. As I stood there looking out at the water, my nerves were not settling down. Keep in mind that I had not swum any distance in my life. The only swimming I had ever done was in a pool or lake, but not any distance at all. Again, I tried to convince myself that since I had run two marathons at 26.2 miles each, a half-mile swim was going to be no problem. Remember overconfidence situation number one? It was back. I was standing there stretching and trying to calm down, and saw a lot of people wearing wetsuits.

I asked someone, "Hey, what is the wetsuit for, to keep you warm in the water?"

They told me, "No, it's to help you float."

I thought to myself, "Oh, that is information that would have been helpful a few weeks ago." I knew that I could use all the help I could get, but I was too far into this thing now to do anything about it.

When my heat was up, I stepped into the water, and it was NOT warm at all. I had a strategy, so I thought. I was going to hang back and let everyone in front of me get out there and then I would start to swim. That way I would be able to swim by myself, behind my heat and in front of the next heat. Some plans are better in theory, including this one.

Once I got about chest-deep in the water, I started to swim. The cold water immediately took my breath away, and within 30 seconds, I knew I was in trouble. I was about 50 yards into this half-mile race and could tell I was not going to make it. I tried to do all the different swimming strokes I could think of, including the doggie paddle, just to keep above the water. I was swimming like a stone.

It wasn't long before the heat after mine caught up to me. There went my strategy of staying in-between heats. I am here to tell you, people swimming in a triathlon do not care at all that you are not a good swimmer. First, I was run over by someone, then the next person kicked me in the ribs. There went any air I had left in my lungs. At that point, I was simply treading water. Somehow, I made my way over to a lifeguard and hung on to their inner tube for dear life. They asked me if I was all right. "Never better," I told them. This was the fourth gut feeling to take note of.

I clung to the tube for a while, as other swimmers continued past me. I regained some strength and breathing ability, and thought I was good to go. Remember what I said about strategies being better in theory? Well, here was another one, because I started swimming again and still had nothing. I made it a little farther and had to find another lifeguard to hang on to for a while. I did this about a half dozen times.

I might have made it about one quarter mile. At the last lifeguard tube, like each time, they asked me how I was doing. Unlike the other times prior, I answered, "Not real good."

The lifeguard said, "You don't look too good. Do you want me to call over a boat to take you in?" I weighed my options. I could hurt my pride, call it a day and have the boat take me in, or I could continue on and have a very good chance to end up at the bottom of the lake. I told them I needed some help.

The lifeguard radioed for a boat, and they fished me out. Riding to shore was the ride of shame. I got out of the boat, and they checked me in the medical tent. The medical person there told me that I did not look so good, and should probably sit down before I fell down. My blood pressure was through the roof, and they said I was close to having the lights turned out, so it was good that I came in. They gave me a snack and some water, and after about 20 minutes they said I was looking better. I returned to my staging area, put my shoes and shirt on, packed my bag, grabbed my bike and off I went, tail between my legs. My first triathlon had just ended, unsuccessfully.

After contemplating the entire experience, and thinking back to the four situations that I should have paid more attention to, I have come to the conclusion that God was warning me about not training properly. It did not matter that I could run 26.2 miles in a marathon. This was swimming. I truly believe that he had me forget my shoes, get lost, and then lose my right shoe. Then, when I still did not listen, he gave an opportunity to call it a day with the first lifeguard.

Unfortunately for me, I did not listen to him on any of the four different occasions. Fortunately for me, we have an all-Loving God that gives us chance after chance, even when we do not listen. My ego was damaged for a while, especially when I got back home and everyone was asking me how it went. I had to tell them I did not even make it out of the swim portion.

God has his own way of telling us (or in this case slapping me side the head), what he wants us to know. He did not want me to fail, so he put all of these obstacles in front of me before I even started the race. Since I was too stubborn to listen, and tried to do it my way, I had to get as far into it as I did before I wised up.

There are still times where I do not really listen as I should, and have to find out the lesson the hard way, but I try to have those times happen as little as possible. I did vow to myself that I was not going to let this situation keep me down, and I would be back. I also told myself that I did not deserve to wear the shirt they gave out, since I did not complete the course. I trained hard, and in September of 2009, I was able to complete my first triathlon. Since then, I have completed three others as well.

This success assures me that God did not want me to fail that day, he was just trying to protect me. He knew I was not ready.
I get asked all the time, especially from those training for their first triathlon, what my advice is. I tell them the same thing: Get your time and training in the water. Don't neglect the biking and running, but focus most on the swim. When you are swimming, relax, take deep breaths, and when you think you are going too slow, go a little slower. Get into a good rhythm that works for you.

My last bit of advice is to pray, LISTEN to God, and most of all, "finish on the top side of the water."

SECTION 3 – Run

Bucket List: Triathlon
by Darcia Kelley

Whenever someone would mention a triathlon, I would think, now there goes an elite athlete. At some point, I started to think I might like to try that someday. My running career had a slow start, but I began to compete in 10K races, and then a 25K. Soon, I thought, I might have a chance someday to fulfill my goal.

I would hear of other friends that competed in this "special elite" race and think, wish I had tried that. However – my BIG challenge came when our town decided they would have a triathlon.
I thought, this is my time! I had been working up to this my whole life, and with God's help, I can do this.

After I told my spinning class that I was going to do the triathlon and also mentioned it to my family, I knew I was committed. At that point, the panic started! Can I do this? What will others say if I mess up? I would probably finish last. Could I actually handle that with my competitive spirit?

I turned to God for direction and peace on this decision. I knew He had always been there for me in the past, so I figured He would help me through this new challenge. During my workouts when the panic thoughts came – "You can never do this" – I would give it up to God. I would pray for strength and say, "God, whatever happens, I trust You to bring me to a successful finish."

Well, I'm here to say, He came through once again! The morning of the race, I felt peace, and I was excited about the challenge. There were many friends there to encourage me, and as I jumped into the cold water. It wasn't worry that surrounded me. It was the peace of

God and the feeling of excitement that I was really in a triathlon!

During the entire race, I didn't push to be number one. I just took the time to enjoy myself, and I pushed to do my best. I didn't worry what place I was in. I just swam, biked, and jogged to the best of my ability all the while knowing that God was with me, giving me the strength and endurance to complete the race.

When I crossed the finish line, I was very tired, but also thankful to God for giving me the opportunity to not only compete in my first-ever Triathlon, but to finish with peace and the feeling of accomplishment ... even though I was next to the last person to finish.

Thank you, God and thanks to the friends that were there for me and encouraged me along the way. Without that, I would never have been able to cross triathlon off my bucket list!

Phil. 4:13 (NASB): "13 I can do all things through Him who strengthens me."

Day 15 – Starting Over

Scripture
Luke 15:11-32

Poem
You revisit an adventure from your childhood
Which caused some fear to manifest

When you get older and try the same thing,
You struggle more than you expect

Trying to overcome old fears
Trying to start over

Starting fresh is like a morning breeze
It's relaxing, and helps provide reflection

Staring an old fear in the face is not easy
Our first reaction is to flee

God wants us to enter into His world
Give him all our fears, worries, and unknowns

Every breath, I pray for his presence
"Help me Oh, Lord, to overcome."

Starting over is hard
The enemy tries to tell us we can't do it:

"You might as well quit
You may have had a new personal best today...

Yet, if you really *had* to do this
You'd fail! Then what would people think of you?"

Over and over, this thought replayed in my head
Even though I went farther than ever before

The voice inside my head states otherwise:
"You are no good."

Here is my prayer:
"Lord, I lay down all my fears and unknowns to you. You sent me
out on this journey because you said so. I'm trying

My best to complete the journey, but the road is not smooth
There are many bumps to overcome. I'm not sure if

I'll ever overcome. Your Grace is sufficient.
I believe that in my heart. I could use an extra dose

Of grace, mercy and hope today,
I'm being attacked for following your Word

The enemy senses my fear and is trying to convince me to quit.
I won't quit, I don't want to let you down.

I know you'll help me through this journey.
Although my Hope is low, it will recover soon.

Enemy, good try! God has blessed me in so many ways
He is helping me grow, at a pace I can handle."

Starting over is not easy, it's challenging
If everything was easy, we wouldn't appreciate our
accomplishments

Thank you Lord, for this gift, and for
The ability to talk to you about anything

Talking to you IS starting over
Thank you for your love.

Every day is a gift.
We start our day with praising you!

Amen!

Story Behind the Poem
For the first nine months of our lives, we swim in the womb. Once
we're out, we struggle with getting back in the water. This was
especially hard for me.

Reading the Bible and living the Bible are two different things.
My hope level got low, learning how to swim and train. Although I
might do 10 laps in the pool one day, I realized that if I had to swim
the course at that point, I'd fail. I still had several months before I
had to do that, however.

My prayer in this story is a real one. I tried a nose plug for the first
time to see if it would help prevent breathing water into my nose.
Starting over with training every time, especially when I trained for
swimming, was not easy. Many times, it's not fun. But when it's a
challenge God gives you, He won't let you fail.

Day 16 – Two feet, neck deep

Scripture

John 7:53-8:11, Luke 18:9-14

Poem

Many years of being a sinner
Many years of scars built up

Day after day, year after year
Sinning away at an uncontrolled pace

Ignoring God, ignoring his will
Doing our own thing as we know best, or so we think

One day something comes along
We cannot control nor do we even know where to start

When you accept God's grace and good news
He takes root in your life, things change

You jump in with both feet
Until you are neck-deep

Trying to do our best to follow God
Every day is a struggle

The changes are obvious to others
People wonder, is the change real?

They have doubts, they think it's fake, and
When your paths cross, insults are spoken

In years past, you would have used colorful words
To explain yourself, to put them in their place

Having God in your heart, changes your heart
Instead of getting mad, you are sad

All you want to do is focus on the real issue
Not be distracted by the perceived falsehood

Based on your understanding of God
Focus on what matters: love, grace and hope

We are neck-deep in our world
And you encounter insults

Some from Christians, some not
Both have the same intention: to judge

Sometimes I wonder how to handle these things
When in doubt, do not respond

Thank you, Lord, for letting me hand over
The struggles of life

In the end, they don't matter
All that matters is our heart and love for you

Through your son Jesus Christ
Who died on that old rugged cross!

Amen!

Story Behind the Poem

I was indirectly called a hypocritical Christian in a discussion forum I responded to. Both non-believers as well as professed Christians were being judgmental of me.

Along the same time, I read two stories by James Watkins:

--"Do those who commit suicide go to heaven?":
http//bit.ly/1dGFpu6

--"Truth and Grace": **http://bit.ly/1j23xXZ**

The two articles posted just above helped me relate to some of the responses I got, which cover unexplainable items.

When you are not happy, being judgmental is OK, according to the world. It lets you express your dissatisfaction and put the blame on someone else. Social media has allowed everyone to have a voice and opinion on a wide variety of sensitive topics. The added benefit of the Internet lets others do this anonymously, and true feelings come out, which means that the words spoken are sharp, direct, or downright nasty. I wasn't sure where to go with being insulted, except hand it over to God and let him deal with it. If it stays on my heart, it will drag me down, and then the enemy gets a foothold.

Day 17 – The Water

Scripture

John 4:14, Matthew 14:22-33, Proverbs 8:29

Poem

Water is something we can't live without
It's a necessity to sustain life

God created water, it's His creation alone
It covers nearly two-thirds of the world

Yet we can't drink most of it because of the salt
I'm not sure the reason, I'm sure it's a good one

God made creatures that can go from salt to fresh water and back
This is a God-given gift to do such a feat

Our first nine months we breathe water
The rest of our life, we could drown from it

Yet we value water so much
Man pays more for houses with lakefront property

When on vacation, we pay more for an ocean view
When the sun rises over the horizon, we want to be close to water

God creates boundaries
So the ocean does not over take the land

Water plays a central role in His great design
During a great storm, Jesus walked on water

He calmed the seas, showing his true power
If someone who can create such a powerful thing

Can command the seas with the sound of his voice
Can make it so important in everything we do

God can help a lowly person like me to overcome the fear of it
I go day after day, moment after moment, wondering

Is this the day it all comes together?
I've questioned God, is this the time my fear leaves me?

I have ultimate faith overcoming my fear will glorify Him
I can't do this on my own, and if I stop before He is done

I could take an opportunity away to glorify Him
Lord, your power and works are awesome

You have used many examples to show your majesty
The seas are unpredictable, dynamic, and a true wonder

These are just a few words that describe your scenery
I have faith in the end of this short journey

You will help guide me through it
My journey is nothing compared to other examples

It is what gives me hope and helps me overcome the fear and
frustration
The next time I feel like I'm in a desert

Help me remember, you are the Giver of Life
As Jesus promised, if you drink His water

You won't thirst anymore
I ask for your help so I can conquer my fear

You are helping overcome deep, old fears
I know you are in control

You will help me, or anyone who asks, in your name
Your love is so deep, we can't understand

Your love is like water: it's clear, powerful and yet gentle
Water is like your words, we can't live without them

Amen!

Story Behind the Poem
This was typed a few weeks before the triathlon.

"This is yet another example of my journey trying to swim. My fear of the water is something as I mentioned was from taking swimming lessons. I can't tell you the fear that came up on a daily basis. I'm not sure the outcome, but I know God is using this journey to document and help me overcome. I know for a fact, without a shadow of a doubt, if it's in His will, I'll make it through. I don't know who it will inspire. If nothing else, it'll help me overcome my fear."

When God laid "water" on my heart, I thought instantly he created water, controls it from taking over the land, had Jesus walk on water to show his power. He can help me overcome my fear of swimming longer distance and help me learn the technique enough to make it a quarter mile. The situation also helped me realize how important water is in human life and examples it's used in, such as baptism. Baptism is a symbol used for new creation, which is washing away the old and bringing in the new. So amazing!

Day 18 – The Waves

Scripture
Mark 4:35-41,Matthew 8:23-27,Luke 8:22-25

Poem
Waves are rhythm to the oceans
They have continual motion

Some are big, some are small
Some are long, some are tall

They carry energy to shape things
They are constant and never-ending

Life is like a wave
With pressure from outside factors

It forms a shape and constantly moves
Until its hits land

It makes a mark and disappears
Another wave right behind does the same thing

Not quite the same way
But with similar force

Over time, wave after wave
Things are shaped and molded

Waves are used to describe things in our lives
"Are we on the same wavelength?"

If we are, things seem to go smoothly
If we are not, things tend to crumble

Much like when waves pound a coastline
Over time, it is shaped and eroded away

There is something left, not like the original
There are times when different waves impact people

They challenge us, they change our lives
Some seem so big, we can't ride them out

We have to become like the thrill seekers
Who want to ride the next big wave

Big wave after big wave
And still stay on top of the board of life

God will be there every step of the way
Providing balance and strength

We might not understand at first
It's scary riding the big wave

We have a constant feeling we are going to fall off
We don't think about succeeding

Fear grips us so tightly
We don't think about anything else

Although it might be larger than we are used to
And when the one wave ends, another wave will be right behind it

Seeking God's glory is the ultimate wave
It starts small and grows

When it hits land, we need to hold on
The enemy will try to keep us down

He will instill fear and doubt
God wants us to grab the board, run back out into the water

Seek another wave, and "get on the same wavelength" as Him
Each stage of life is like a wave

We get going and sometimes get knocked off
We pick up ourselves, get back up and try again

The enemy is as persistent as waves are to a shoreline
He'll try to shape us to his likening, which is opposite of God's

We need to put our faith in riding God's wave
There will be many over time, but one thing is for sure

God's waves and wavelength are two things we want to be on
Looking at it from an eternal view, you'll be glad you did

Hang on tight while riding the surfboard of life
One day we'll finish riding

To walk into Glory and hang with God
Forever and ever!

Amen!

Story Behind the Poem

On the last day of vacation, just before we were ready to head home, I looked out the window and noticed the waves. Almost instantly, I knew the good Lord wanted to use waves as a story.

The day before, I found out my Dad was going in for his first cancer treatment. I knew it was going to cause a new wave of anxiety. For my Dad, it's another wave to ride.

After reading about waves and how they worked, I realized how we used the words "waves" and "wavelength" to describe things in our lives.

Day 19 – The Unknown

Scripture
Acts 2

Poem
One day removed from many unknowns
Almost had a meltdown

So frustrated
I tried to hand it off to the Lord

The unknown kept creeping back
The unknown had a tight grip

A quick nap to help forget
The frustration that set in

A mental block was so tall
It felt taller than a skyscraper

No handles to grasp
No lifeline to hold on to

It was a stalemate
No idea where to go next

In unfamiliar territory
Trying to reason

A quick run to help with stress
Could not resolve the unknown

A good night's sleep interrupted
The enemy would not let up

Planting seeds of doubt
Over a situation that wasn't real

The doubt and unknown remain
To this day, and I'm not sure what is next

The Lord is engaged in the unknown
Everything laid at his feet

I have to wait for a response
Meanwhile, I find strength in sharing

I know it will be all right in the end
There is structured work ahead

When encountering something unknown and foreign
People want the easy way out

I'm no exception
Fast and faster are the rule of the day

Succeeding in this world requires others
Which involves trust and patience

Everyone involved has a willing heart
Lord, once again, I hand you my troubles

Please shine your light once again on the unknown
So it will eventually lose, darkness fades when the light shines.

Amen!

Story Behind the Poem
I am a task-oriented, yet unstructured person. Handling structured
tasks is something I don't enjoy and is a lot of work and mental

effort. My personality is also the type that looks for the easy way out of a situation.

Anything difficult and hard to maintain isn't worth doing in my opinion. I struggle with work when it involves collecting, cataloging and structuring information (i.e., data entry). Once the initial excitement is gone, the work remains, and it's a mental struggle for me.

All and all, it's another opportunity to give glory to God, because he is testing me. I don't want to let Him down. I'll do my best and involve Him in prayer. I forget the specifics of this story, yet have had this struggle in the past. Regardless how long you walk with the Lord, challenges will occur and unknowns will happen, but as long as you lean on the Lord and do it with the right intentions, usually things will work out.

Day 20 – Wetsuit

Scripture
1 Corinthians 10:13

Poem
There are times in life
When risks are taken with the result unknown

We face the day with hope that things will work out
We try and learn from our mistakes

After a person makes enough mistakes
They learn to survive and make do

They have enough mental resources to finish the day's tasks
Rarely is there anything left over

Hope is a God-given source of comfort
Doubt is a good motivator

When preparing for anything in life
You research how to do it

Through trial and error
You discover techniques and shortcuts

While performing the task
You know there are ways to do it better

There can be costs involved;
You're not sure the investment will pay off

That is part of the adventure some would say
God wants us to put forth the effort by faith

Many will tell you the blessings didn't happen beforehand
Only when the effort was given

Did God come alongside
He was patiently waiting for us to take the first step

The appreciation brings a different perspective
As a person gets older, it takes more to surprise them

They know to not expect too much
This goes for working hard

The outcome doesn't usually live up to the hype
There are occasions when

God will bless the effort in a special way
Appreciate everything in its own special way

Regardless of your experience, be thankful
God will surprise, we just have to wait and see

Put forth the effort, don't expect anything in return
When blessings do come

That will make them that much sweeter
Because they come from the Creator

What do you believe?

Amen!

Story Behind the Poem

Working in computers has taught me to *really* know and
understand the things I'm working on. I'm expected to know a
process, any associating procedures, and any technology to help

solve the problem thoroughly. When you work at something long enough, everything has its shortcomings, and nothing is perfect. Secondly, I tend not to expect too much, because I know failures are frequent.

Although I was training to swim, as I've said in many of the poems and stories, I didn't expect to complete the swim portion of the triathlon. Faith alone is how I expected to complete the swim portion. After a church friend mentioned a website renting wetsuits, I took the leap of faith. To my surprise, it made a huge difference. My training and the wetsuit together then allowed me to have more than enough stamina to complete the swim portion.

Maybe as a person ages and has a few failures, their expectations are lower. The fact that I was able to use a wetsuit to overcome much of my fears is a clear reminder that God will come up big, in unexpected ways. You just need faith.   Great risks mean great rewards, as long as it is God-inspired.

Day 21 – Victory

Scripture
1 Corinthians 15

Poem
When a journey is started
Hopes are high to complete the task successfully

The definition of success is subjective
If you look from the world's point of view

The meaning can vary
One thing for sure

Victory is the standard the world judges
No room for second place

The non-winners should just fade away
They shouldn't even try again

We know non-winners are winners too in a different way
They gave their best effort, trained and hope to win

Although they didn't win, just finishing is worth something
Completion can be a victory

When we start a God-inspired journey
The God-driven gifts and motivation are provided by the Creator

No need to do this anymore on our own
God gets in the driver's seat

We can try to be a back-seat driver
This will do no good, because God has a plan

His plans are different from the world
Winning and being victorious are for all, not just one

It took just one to make God's grace happen
Jesus gave us victory over death

He made eternal life a free gift to all
Although the road was tough

Continue on the journey through the finish line
In eternity. Jesus, who provided the way

He will be standing there waiting to congratulate you
And celebrate in your victory!

Amen!

Story Behind the Poem
I was sitting in church after finishing the triathlon, thinking, what is next? About the second or third song, the word victory popped in my head. God provided me "God-driven gifts," which means giving me the drive, opportunity and protection to complete a task.
I finished my first triathlon in 1 hour, 59 minutes, 17 seconds. The winner, in comparison, did the entire event in 57 minutes. The distance was a quarter-mile mile swim, an 11.8-mile bike ride, and a 5k run (3.1 miles).

My bib number was 58, which, if you add the numbers together, is 13. My place was 158th, which ironically also contains the number 58. I averaged 12.4 miles per hour on the bike, which was a record for me, and 15 minutes in the swim portion, which was 1-2 minutes faster than my regular training time. The run was about what I averaged normally, 39 minutes.

There were several times that I felt defeated. Five months prior, a good friend was at the pool for my first time, and she mentioned, "I could hear some water splashing around, I wasn't real impressed." I found out a few days prior that I had a double hernia, and running was pretty painful. God was patient and kept me healthy enough to keep training. And I was terrified to swim, although I didn't want to potentially miss an opportunity to provide him glory and complete the triathlon.

I had many helpers along the way who provided exercises, drills, and advice that helped. The wetsuit in particular made all the difference! I'm sure many others would agree that God has helped me get better. I would agree that in the end, God gave me the feeling of victory, not defeat.

I hope if you are reading this and struggling, take heart. Jesus conquered the world and can walk alongside you to help you achieve success; success not from a world view, but from God's view.

Reflection

(These words were originally part of the Victory poem. My editor pointed out the words these summarize the entire book.
After removing them, the Victory poem was even more powerful.
After separating out the words, I see she was right!)

Here are some words to ponder in your training. Hope they help!

The training was more than I've ever done
Overcoming obstacles I always feared

A small still voice stated
Forget Everything and Race (F.E.A.R)

Do the best you can with the talents provided
Swim, Bike, Run

All three in one
Do not measure against the world

Use my form of measurement to determine the outcome
After each event, celebrate and continue on

Even if something tries to stop you.

Credits and References

- Couch to 5K app - **http://bit.ly/1b9a3EM**
- Punxsutawney Phil info - **http://bit.ly/lwBth8**
- One of the songs I heard was from **http://www.group1crew.com**
- The radio station I listen to the most is Smile.fm (**http://bit.ly/1gq9wDZ**). The "Diceman" asked the question "Who do you trust?"
- Day 16 - Story **http://bit.ly/18Og5hK**
  James Watkins is an author and speaker.

About the Author

Steve Schofield was saved in August of 2005, and began writing poems shortly after that to deal with life's stresses. He lives in West Michigan with his wife Cindy and their three sons. They are active members of the Greenville Community Church.

Steve is an IT professional, and has long been a self-described "internet geek," so he used that skill to develop a couple of online applications that fund his writing habit.

He is the author of two other Christian devotionals:

52 Pickup: These Are the Words I Give to You to Share with Everyone (ISBN-13: 978-1449773045)
- Paperback – **http://amzn.to/UiExjv**
- Kindle Version – **http://amzn.to/10q38W1**

Remember the Nails: 40 Days of Doing Something Uncomfortable on Purpose (ISBN-13 : 978-0984651696)
- Paperback – **http://amzn.to/1e2txNO**
- Kindle Version – **http://amzn.to/11FE8fh**

"I give thanks to God for using me to share these poems and stories. He has inspired me to tell them, and there were many times I could sense the Holy Spirit assisting me in my writing. There certainly is nothing like having our Creator speaks directly to you; words can't describe it! I only hope that I can help someone else along their own path, whether they are Christian yet or not. I feel this is my purpose, and if I only reach one person... that would be enough."

The author is also available for speaking engagements and other events. Visit his website (http://www.52pickup.co/) for more information.